The Collector's Encyclopedia of

Occupied Japan
Collectibles

Fourth Series

By Gene Florence

COLLECTOR BOOKS

A Division of Schroeder Publishing Co., Inc.

The current values in this book should be used only as a guide. They are not intended to set prices, which vary from one section of the country to another. Auction prices as well as dealer prices vary greatly and are affected by condition as well a demand. Neither the Author nor the Publisher assumes responsibility for any losses that might be incurred as a result of consulting this guide.

FOREWORD

"Made in Occupied Japan" has been a magic phrase to some collectors for years, but as many new collectors join the fraternity, the supply of pieces marked with those magic words decreases daily. In the three years since my **Third** book, I have experienced a deluge of letters wanting to know more about this collecting field!

For those readers who have not seen the previous editions, I will reiterate some basic information.

All items made in Japan (from the beginning of our occupation at the end of World War II until April 28, 1952, when the occupation ended), that were to be exported to the United States had to be marked in one of four ways: "Japan", "Made in Occupied Japan", "Occupied Japan" or "Made in Japan." You can see that if all the markings were used equally or nearly so, still only about half of the items imported into the United States would have been marked with the magic words for collectors, "Made in OCCUPIED JAPAN." Thus, too, you will find that there are many similar or like items which you will find marked only "Japan" or "Made in Japan." There is no way of proving these were actually made in "Occupied Japan." (For the sake of brevity, capital letters "MIOJ" and "OJ" will be used throughout the remainder of this book to mean "Made in Occupied Japan" or "Occupied Japan.") I must emphasize that unless an item actually says OCCUPIED in some form, it can not be considered to be such. The only exception to that rule would apply to items found in original containers such as boxes or cartons where the container is marked "MIOJ" while the items within are only marked "Japan." These items must always stay with the original container to be collected as OCCUPIED. From past observation and correspondence with collectors over the years, it is obvious that a large number of items imported from Japan during this time were marked on the containers only; and, of course, many of these original containers have been discarded. The original consumers did not care whether an item was marked "OJ" or not. These were governmental policies. It is speculated that only a small percentage of the larger, finer wares were themselves marked "MIOJ." The dearth of these larger marked pieces today makes them avidly sought by collectors and very desirable to own. If you have a choice between buying one quality piece or several smaller items, I recommend you consider buying the one.

All items in this book are marked OJ or MIOJ unless noted. If no color is listed, then the mark is black. All other colors and markings will be listed in parentheses. Measurements to the nearest eighth of an inch are given for the first piece in the row, and if needed, additional measurements in that row will be added. This should help you in pricing similar pieces of OJ.

Be aware that there are counterfeits available and you can read about these in my **Third** book. I have not heard from the Occupied Japan Club in California in the last three years, but there is another club on the East coast which has an annual show! You can get additional information by sending a SASE to: O.J. Club c/o Florence Archambalt, 29 Freeborn Street, Dept GF, Newport, RI 02840. Dues are $15.00 yearly and there is a monthly newsletter.

ACKNOWLEDGMENTS

A special thanks to my family for pitching in and helping make this book possible. It all started with Marc, my son, and Cathy going to Wisconsin to pick up a 10,000 piece collection of Occupied Japan last July when I had my arm in a sling with a broken wrist. They had to do the wrapping, packing and loading since I was incapacitated. Marc decided for sure that Dad was crazy when it all would not fit in my van and a second trip had to be made over Labor Day!

Grannie Bear, Cathy, Sibyl and I then spent a week at home unwrapping, sorting and packing this collection (and all the other MIOJ I had purchased over the last two years) for the photography session. Getting categories together and eliminating items already shown in the three previous books was a gigantic six day, dawn to midnight, undertaking!

The photography for the book was done by Tom Clouser of Curtis and Mays in Paducah, Kentucky. At the studio we were aptly aided in arranging this into some further semblance of order by Steve Quertermous, Jane White and Teri Hatch while Cathy had all the "fun" she wanted in unwrapping, recording the markings and measuring the pieces in each photograph before wrapping them again. We hope you enjoy all our efforts to show you a little corner of the "Occupied Japan World."

PRICING

All prices in this book are retail. The last thing I do for any book is to go over the prices, updating any new developments that may occur after the writing is finished. This is not as critical in "OJ" as in other fields of collecting, but with publishing lead times as they are today, I want you to know that the prices are current. I sell hundreds of pieces of "MIOJ" in my shop each year with one sale in excess of seven thousand dollars. I only mention this to let you know that the prices listed are not "hoped-for" prices, but actual selling prices. Many of the items shown will now be for sale in my shop; and by the time you read this, most of the best items will already have new homes. I try to spread the sale of the better pieces over a period of time, but if someone says, "I will take them all," then they own them!

You will see higher prices for "OJ" than are listed in this book; I say that for the lady in California who lectured me at length that I priced OJ way too cheaply. I am aware that you will find a few pieces cheaper than those listed. I say that for the man in Pennsylvania, who wrote the same week the lady called, to say I priced OJ so high that nobody in the world could get those prices out of it. Yard and garage sales as well as auctions are good sources for finding bargains on "OJ," but more and more people are becoming aware of those magic words "MIOJ." Be prepared to pay a fair price and hope to find a bargain or two. You will see the same overpriced items time and time again in your travels. Remember that someday you may find the same item at an affordable price. If not, you can chuckle to yourself, as I do, over the prices you see the item not selling for again at shows or in a shop. Unfortunately, people with a little bit of knowledge about "MIOJ" sometimes think that they have a gold mine if they own it.

This book is meant as a guide only. They buyer and the seller determine actual worth. If a mutually agreeable price can be arranged between these two, then that is the price no matter what the book says! I buy and sell. I have to make those decisions often. Many times I leave pieces I would love to have but believe the price is out of line. You have to determine your limits as a collector. I repeat, these prices are meant to be a good, general guide.

Prices are listed as retail; thus, if you want to sell some of your collection to a dealer, you will have to discount them. Most dealers are willing to pay 50% to 60% of the retail price of most items. Common pieces or hard to sell items will be discounted more. Remember the better the piece or the more unusual it is, the more collectors will be looking for it.

Collectors are looking for mint items. The prices listed in this book are for mint condition items. That means having all the parts; no cracks, chips or glued pieces are acceptable. Unless it is very unusual and hard to get, there is little value to damaged pieces.

As in the previous books, I have included a price range for each piece. Several collectors have told me, "I buy at low book and sell at high." Be your own judge. It is your money and only you determine how you spend it–unless you are married that is!

TABLE OF CONTENTS

ANGELS and CHERUBS

As we begin this fourth journey into "Occupied Japan" collecting, I would like to reiterate (for those of you who don't read introductions) that if no color is listed for the mark, then the marking is in **BLACK**. All pieces shown are marked with the word **"OCCUPIED"** in some form. That word may, at times, be misspelled; but each piece has to be marked **"OCCUPIED"** for it to be considered a collectible of this genre. Most pieces are listed by size (as they were in the last book). In rows where all pieces are much the same height, the first piece in the row is sized for reference. I received many letters asking me to continue that practice.

As a matter of reference, in this picture angels are winged and the cherubs are not winged.

The top row contains two exceptional figurines on the right. These are probably parts of a set. The last three rows contain examples of sets that can be assembled with some searching. Matching the base designs of these miniature vases, as well as remembering which instrument your little angel has might give you a headache; so make lists or take pictures of what you have to carry with you as you look; then just relax and enjoy the fun of looking for the others!

Top Row:
    1st, Cherub, 5" (red) — $10.00-12.50
    2nd, Cherub, 3⅝" (red) — 6.00- 8.00
    3rd, Angel w/mandolin, 6⅜" — 17.50-20.00
    4th, Cherub w/horn, 6⅝" (red) — 22.50-25.00
    5th, Angel pair, 6" (red) — 30.00-35.00

Second Row:
    1st, 3rd, (red) and 4th, (red) Angels — 6.00- 8.00 ea.
    2nd, Cherub, pair (red) — 15.00-17.50
    5th, Angel w/lattice basket ("Lenwile China Set,"
       "Ardalt 62020") — 17.50-20.00

Third Row:
    1st, Angel w/mandolin, 2⅝" — 4.00- 5.00
    2nd, Angel w/drum — 8.00-10.00
    3rd, Cherub, pair w/grapes (red) — 15.00-17.50
    4th, 5th and 6th, Angels w/instruments, vase, 4" (red) — 7.50-10.00 ea.

Fourth Row:
    1st-7th, Angels w/instruments, vase, 4" (red) — 7.50-10.00 ea.

Fifth Row:
    1st-4th, Angels seated w/instruments, 2⅛" (red) — 4.00- 5.00 ea.
    5th-7th, Angels seated w/instruments, 3" (red) — 7.50-10.00 ea.
    8th, Angel seated w/ guitar, 2½" (red) — 5.00- 6.50

ANIMALS – DOGS

There are beaucoup collectors of dog figurines; many of whom know nothing about collecting Occupied Japan. Thus, collectors of dog figurines push the prices of Occupied Japan dogs upward. This comes from the demand of overlapping collecting fields.

Nice quality and special breeds of dogs are in demand. There seem to be few French poodles or bulldogs found, but there are many collectors searching for these. Next most collectible are the Scottie dogs; more of these are available with diligent searching. German Shepherds and any dog which looks similar to the household pet are the next most in demand.

Top Row:

1st, Seated dog, 4⅜"	$20.00-22.50
2nd, "Luster," dog (red)	10.00-12.50
3rd, Gray and white	10.00-12.50
4th, Bird dogs (blue Circle **T**)	30.00-35.00
5th, Standing dog, 7⅛"	17.50-20.00

Second Row:

1st, 4th, 5th and 8th, ("Ucagco China" w/emblem)	15.00-17.50 ea.
2nd and 6th, (Circle **T**)	12.50-15.00 ea.
3rd, Collie	10.00-12.50
7th, Setter (Circle **T**), souvenir Grand Rapids, Wisc.	12.50-15.00

Third Row:

1st, 2nd and 7th, dogs	7.50-10.00 ea.
3rd, Scottie	10.00-12.50
4th and 6th, (**T** over **M**)	8.00-10.00 ea.
5th, Standing dog (Impressed Occupied Japan)	10.00-12.50

Fourth Row:

1st, Standing (**T** over **M**)	10.00-12.50
2nd, Scottie ("Ucagco China" w/emblem)	12.50-15.00
3rd, Black and White (Circle **T**)	20.00-22.50
4th and 5th, Celluloid Scotties	6.00- 8.00 ea.
6th, Terrier	10.00-12.50
7th, Scottie (Circle **T**)	12.50-15.00
8th, Small (very detailed)	10.00-12.50

Fifth Row:

1st, 6th and 7th, groups (red)	8.00-10.00 ea.
2nd, Big ears	6.00- 8.00
3rd and 4th, Basket dogs, 3"	10.00-12.50 ea.
5th, Scotties in cart	12.50-15.00

ANIMALS.

The variety of animals found marked "Occupied Japan" is illustrated here, although I might get a few Science teachers upset by including butterflies, clams and lobsters in this category. I had to chuckle at my wife Cathy's notes from the photography session. The large mouth bass shown next to the angel fish was listed as a shark.

The pride of lions in the top row and the trio of elephants on the second row right side are some of the better Occupied Japan animals I have seen outside of cats and dogs.

The most unusual has to be the dark brown "snow baby" type monkey holding bananas behind his back in the fourth row. The first monkey in the fourth row needs a piano for his outstretched hands.

Top Row:

1st, Lion pride, 4⅛" high (blue)	$ 30.00-35.00
2nd, Lion	5.00- 6.00
3rd, Pig (blue)	8.00-10.00
4th, Seal (blue)	6.00- 8.00
5th, Squirrel (Circle **T**)	10.00-12.50
6th, Squirrel, pair (blue Circle **T**)	30.00-35.00

Second Row:

1st, Green elephant, 3¾", "Ucagco China" w/emblem	15.00-17.50
2nd, Small brown elephant (green)	7.50-10.00
3rd, Grayish-white elephant, 4" (red)	15.00-17.50
4th and 5th, Pink elephants (blue)	4.00- 5.00 ea.
6th, Brown elephant (brown)	10.00-12.50
7th, Red elephant (blue)	5.00- 6.00
8th-10th, Elephant family set	50.00-75.00
Large (Impressed mark on foot)	20.00-25.00
Medium (marked same)	15.00-20.00
Small (Impressed mark on tummy)	12.50-15.00

Third Row:

1st, 2nd and 5th, Roosters (red)	5.00- 6.00 ea.
3rd, Large rooster, 3½"	8.00-10.00
4th, Chicken family	17.50-20.00
6th, Butterfly	6.00- 8.00

Fourth Row:

1st, Monkey missing piano, 3⅛" (red)	8.00-10.00
w/piano	12.50-15.00
2nd and 3rd, Monkeys w/instruments	12.50-15.00
4th, Monkey w/horn (blue)	6.00- 8.00
5th, Monkey w/dark brown suit (red circle w/cross)	30.00-35.00
6th, Three monkey set (red)	8.00-10.00
7th, Rabbit w/drum (red)	12.50-15.00
8th, Rabbit w/egg (red)	6.00- 8.00
9th, Lobster (red)	17.50-20.00

Fifth Row:

1st, Fish (brown)	6.00- 8.00
2nd, Fish in weeds	5.00- 6.00
3rd and 6th, (red Pico)	6.00- 8.00 ea.
4th, Clams open or closed (paper label)	5.00- 6.00 ea.
5th, Bisque bass (blue)	8.00-10.00
7th, White fish (red)	5.00- 6.00

ASH TRAYS and CIGARETTE BOXES

Collectors in many fields seem to avoid buying smoker's items, lately. This has caused a drop in prices. Personally speaking, I would hope that all collectors could give up smoking! (Coming from the tobacco state of Kentucky, I might be hanged in effigy, for saying that!)

Even though there has been some avoidance of smoking items, there are still fascinating and beautiful accessory items being found marked "Occupied Japan." The swans shown on the top row make an attractive set. The cigarette box is unmarked. The smaller swans are individual ash trays.

Some cigarette box lids have been turned to better show their beauty. Normally, there are two ash trays to go with each box. To conserve space, only one shown in most cases.

Top Row:

1st-4th, Swan set (gold "Chipusa" w/cross)	$75.00-100.00
Small swan	12.50- 15.00 ea.
Large swan	30.00- 40.00
Swan box	20.00- 30.00

Second Row:

1st, Black cigarette box w/floral top (red **T** over **M**)	22.50- 25.00
2nd, Cigarette box w/applied roses (red)	20.00- 22.50
3rd, Black cigarette box w/floral top (yellow **T** over **M**)	22.50- 25.00

Third Row:

1st, Ash tray w/bird (blue)	12.50- 15.00
2nd-4th, Ash trays for above boxes	8.00- 10.00 ea.
5th, Fish ash tray (red "Ucagco China" w/emblem)	7.50- 10.00

Fourth Row:

1st, Black cigarette box w/orchid ("Waco")	25.00- 30.00
2nd-4th, Children ash trays (blue)	5.00- 6.00 ea.
5th, Pagoda scene box (**T** over **M**)	25.00- 30.00

Fifth Row:

1st, House on lake scene ash tray (red)	7.50- 10.00
2nd, Flower cigarette holder (gold "Ucagco China" w/emblem)	17.50- 20.00
3rd, Chamber pot "For old butts and ashes" (blue)	5.00- 6.00
4th, Swan w/tail cigarette rest (brown)	6.00- 8.00

For Old Butts and Ashes

ASH TRAYS, BANKS, BELLS, BOOKENDS, etc.

Again, cigarette items as well as other smoker's items have fallen out of favor with collectors in recent years. Only unusual shaped or superbly decorated pieces have been in vogue.

However, the rest of the items shown here are all highly desirable to collectors. There are few banks found, since most had to broken to remove the contents. Bells have always been collected; and Occupied Japan bells are no exception.

This page was stacked with all sorts of "**B**" words besides the banks. Bird cage feeder, baseball items, bells, bookends and a boxer added to the repertoire. The baseball items are avidly sought by sports memorabilia collectors. Baseball card collecting has launched collecting into many other baseball related collectibles.

There is a colonial lady to match the colonial man candle holder shown on the end of the bottom row. I just couldn't find her this time.

Top Row:
1st, Embossed rose tray (brown **W** in wreath)	$ 4.00- 5.00
2nd, Floral tray (green)	2.50- 4.00
3rd, Cigarette holder ("Berkshire Fine China")	4.00- 5.00
4th, "Wedgwood" type ash tray, white w/blue	10.00-12.50
5th, Curled leaf ("Chubu China")	2.50- 4.00
6th, "Wedgwood" type ash tray ("Pico")	10.00-12.50

Second Row:
1st, Potty "Seat of Nation Ladies"	5.00- 6.00
2nd, Same, "Seat of Nation Gents"	5.00- 6.00
3rd, Hand (red **S** in circle)	4.00- 5.00
4th, Clown w/heart (part of bridge set)	2.00- 3.00
5th and 7th, Floral trays (red)	2.00- 3.00 ea.
6th, Teapot (blue)	2.50- 4.00
8th, Leaf (gold "Ucagco China" w/emblem)	2.50- 4.00

Third Row:
1st and 2nd, Pig bank set (smaller unmarked)	30.00-35.00
3rd and 6th, Pig banks (red)	25.00-35.00 ea.
4th, Pig bank	8.00-10.00
5th, Elephant bank (blue)	25.00-35.00

Fourth Row:
1st-3rd, Baseball players (red)	15.00-17.50 ea.
4th, Metal fielder's glove ash tray (embossed mark)	10.00-12.50
5th and 7th, Bells (red)	20.00-22.50 ea.
6th, Dutch girl bell	17.50-20.00

Fifth Row:
1st, Owl bird cage feeder	10.00-12.50
2nd and 3rd, Bookend (red)	35.00-40.00 pr.
4th and 5th, Dutch Bookend (red)	35.00-40.00 pr.
6th, Boxer	10.00-12.50
7th, Colonial male candle holder (red)	20.00-22.50

BABY BUGGIES, CLOWNS and CRADLES

I know one of the first questions I will get will concern the category of "baby buggies, clowns and cradles." You would have to visit a photography session some time to understand. Pictures are laid out in your mind and categories are combined for the best ways to display what we wish to show. Alphabetically, makes the most sense, but sometimes there are few pieces found that fit adequately into this frame of reference. The "baby buggies, clowns and cradles" filled up a picture in a space where it was needed at the time. See, you thought it was a stroke of insanity, but it was just "luck of the draw."

Collectors of clowns are driving up the prices on these rapidly (particularly figurines). I have seen some wild prices on some great clown salt and pepper shakers recently! The clown and drum sets in the fourth row are each different. The drum is one shaker while the clown is the other!

Top Row:
1st, Blue buggy planter, 5¼" (arch symbol)	$ 8.00-10.00
2nd and 3rd, Buggies w/head on side	12.50-15.00 ea.
4th, Same as 1st only pink	8.00-10.00

Second Row:
1st, Reclining clown (red)	30.00-35.00
2nd, Clown doing hand stand (red)	30.00-35.00
3rd, Clown in striped suit, 5¼" ("Ucagco China" w/emblem; red)	35.00-40.00
4th, Clown playing bass fiddle (red)	15.00-17.50
5th, Clown, 5" ("Mocco"; red)	15.00-17.50
6th, Reclining clown ("Ucagco China" w/emblem; red)	30.00-35.00

Third Row:
1st-3rd, Cradles w/child	12.50-15.00 ea.
4th, Buggy w/bird on side	4.00- 5.00
5th, Small (doll house size) buggy, 1⅞" (blue)	5.00- 6.00

Fourth Row:
1st, Clown playing saxophone (brown)	8.00-10.00
2nd-4th, Clown w/vase	6.00- 8.00 ea.
5th and 6th, Clown on drum salt and pepper set	30.00-35.00 set

Fifth Row:
1st-3rd, Buggies w/head in brown, pink and blue	12.50-15.00 ea.
4th, "Hummel like" girl w/black buggy (red)	17.50-20.00

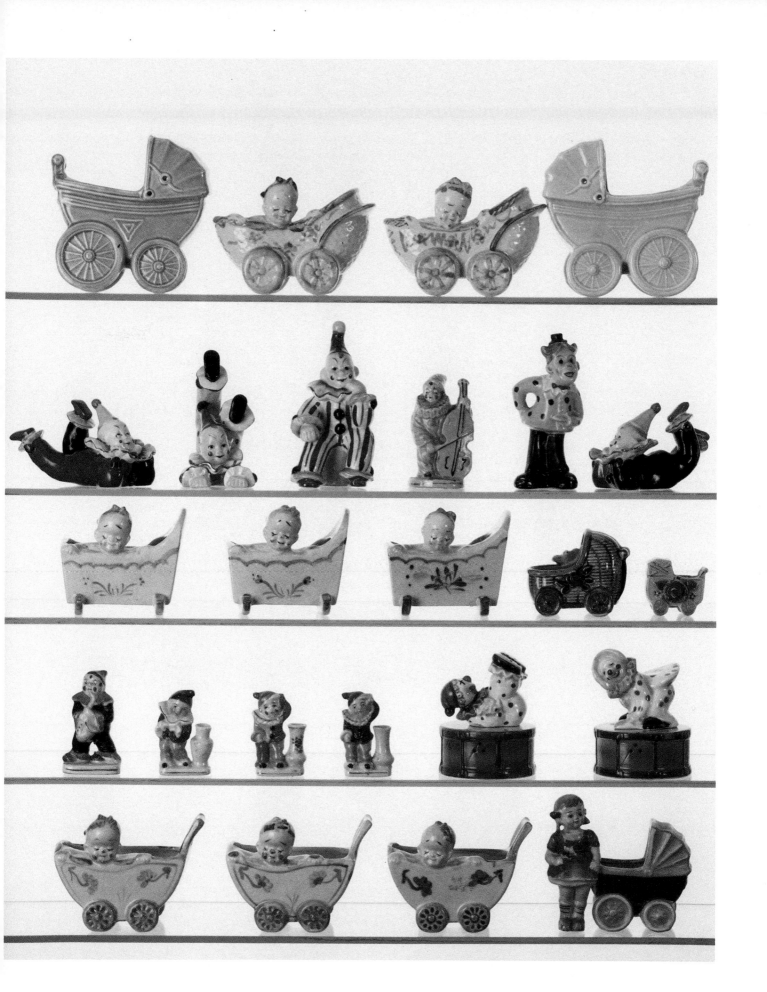

BIRDS and FEATHERED FRIENDS

Collectors of bird figurines can find some quality ones here as well as some "junque" types. Some have vivid detail while others are difficult to even determine a species.

The many goose poses in the fourth row are as varied as the colors, but most are yellow feathered on the breast which makes them an unknown species to me. Maybe there were few Canadian geese available in Japan to pose for figurines. Those who enjoy a Christmas goose probably have never tried to dry pluck one in the kitchen as I once tried, much to Cathy's dismay.

I have been told that the ducks on the bottom row are representative examples of "Donald Duck," but I have never documented that. The three on the far right look like an earlier version, but not the versions seen in my lifetime. Perhaps some early cartoons from before the war made it to Japan.

Top Row:
1st, Large bird, 7⅞", on branch (brown)	$25.00-30.00
2nd, Small bird on branch (blue)	2.00- 3.00
3rd, Pair of birds (blue)	10.00-12.50
4th, Pair of birds (red)	10.00-12.50
5th, Large bird on planter, 7¾" (red)	25.00-30.00

Second Row:
1st, Colorful bird (red)	10.00-12.50
2nd, Bird bending (blue)	12.50-15.00
3rd, Bird on branch (blue "Ucagco China" w/emblem)	10.00-12.50
4th, Small birds on branch (red)	2.00- 3.00
5th, Blue bird (blue **T**)	4.00- 5.00
6th, Green bird (brown)	6.00- 8.00

Third Row:
1st, 2nd, 3rd and 5th, Stork or pelican (red)	6.00- 8.00 ea.
4th, Swan	5.00- 6.00
6th, Small winged bird (red)	6.00- 8.00
7th-9th, Small birds (red)	4.00- 5.00 ea.

Fourth Row:
1st-6th, Geese	6.00- 7.50 ea.

Fifth Row:
1st-8th, Musical "Donald Ducks" (red or blue)	8.00-10.00 ea.
9th-11th, Musical long billed ducks (red)	6.00- 8.00 ea.

BISQUE

Many bisque figurines made in Occupied Japan rival those made in Germany in quality and detail. Other Occupied Japan bisque figurines are poorly designed and of poor quality. It is the finer detailed figurines that collectors now avidly seek. Many of these statues can be purchased at prices less than those of today's newly made figurines. At least with the Occupied Japan pieces there is collectibility behind them and their value will not decrease the moment you take them home.

Many couples married during the occupation time period and kept the bride and groom figures poised upon their wedding cakes as souvenirs of the occasion. These are often marked "Occupied Japan." You can see two different sizes here, but the taller (6⅛") seems to be rarely found.

The matching planters in the middle of the second row have a hole on the back for attaching these to the wall. I suspect that was the cause of the demise of many of these!

Remember that there is no glaze on bisque pieces, so do not try to remove marks with lighter fluid or any other solvent as you may destroy an old mark.

Top Row:
1st, Bride and groom, 6⅛"	$30.00- 35.00
2nd, Lady w/basket, 6½"	25.00- 30.00
3rd, Plaque, 6¼" (red)	25.00- 30.00
4th, Plaque, 6¾" (red)	35.00- 40.00
5th, Man holding hat, 6"	22.50- 25.00
6th, Lady w/dog and gun	22.50- 25.00

Second Row:
1st, Dancers, 3", (red)	10.00- 12.50
2nd, Bride and groom, 4¼" ("New Star")	20.00- 22.50
3rd and 4th, Planter pair, 5¼" (red "Paulux")	115.00 pr.
5th, Child playing accordion, 2¾" (impressed mark)	10.00- 12.50
6th, Boy w/puppy (**M** over **C** in circle)	12.50- 15.00

Third Row:
1st, Man w/umbrella, 3⅝" (red)	12.50- 15.00
2nd and 7th, Man and Woman	10.00- 12.50 ea.
3rd, Lady, 5" (red)	12.50- 15.00
4th, Couple, 5⅝" (red)	30.00- 35.00
5th, Seated couple w/dog, 3⅝"	12.50- 15.00
6th, Wall pocket, 2⅜"	8.00- 10.00
8th, Child w/instrument (impressed mark on back)	10.00- 12.50

Fourth Row:
1st and 2nd, Planter couple, 6¼"	30.00- 40.00 pr.
3rd and 4th, Planters, 6" ("Paulux")	75.00 pr.
5th, Fisherman, 7" (gold "Ucagco China" w/emblem)	30.00- 35.00
6th, Man w/cape, 6" ("Hadson")	20.00- 22.50

BISQUE (Cont.)

As on the previous page, there are some super quality figurines shown here. Most of these better figurines are marked Paulux. That company may have made some lesser quality figures, but most of the ones I have seen over the years have been the "creme de la creme."

Normally, I find planters rather unattractive and boring, but most of the planters shown in the bisque section will add to, rather than detract from, a collection of Occupied Japan.

The "Andrea" horse and rider in the bottom row stands 10¼" high and is a magnificent example of bisque Occupied Japan.

Prices for individual figurines are half the lowest price of the pair!

Top Row:

1st, Lady planter, 6" (red "Paulux")	$ 75.00
2nd and 3rd, Cart planters, 7" (red "Paulux")	150.00 pr.
4th and 5th, Couple, 6½" (red) (lady unmarked)	25.00- 35.00 pr.

Second Row:

1st and 2nd, Tree vases, 4½"	17.50- 20.00 pr.
3rd, Dancer, (red)	6.00- 8.00
4th and 5th, Musicians, 4½" (red)	12.50- 15.00 ea.
6th, Drummer, 4½" (brown)	12.50- 15.00
7th, Boy w/rabbit	10.00- 12.50
8th and 9th, Couple, 4¼" (red)	17.50- 20.00 pr.

Third Row:

1st and 2nd, Couple, 5⅜" (red)	25.00- 35.00 pr.
3rd, Kid couple planter, (red "Paulux")	40.00- 45.00
4th, Sunflower kids, (red "Paulux")	45.00- 50.00
5th and 6th, Colonial couple, (brown)	30.00- 35.00 pr.

Fourth Row:

1st and 2nd, Couple with dogs, 7⅛" (**L D** in emblem)	75.00- 85.00 pr.
3rd, Horse w/rider, 10¼" ("Andrea," H.P.)	150.00-175.00
4th and 5th, Couple, 7¼" ("Paulux")	65.00- 75.00 pr.

Remember that there is no glaze on bisque pieces, so do not try to remove marks with lighter fluid as any other solvent as you may destroy an old mark.

CELLULOID

Celluloid pieces are difficult to find undamaged. Remember that prices below are for undamaged specimens. Slightly damaged pieces will only fetch about half of the prices shown, and badly damaged pieces are rarely collected unless unusual.

Remember that celluloid is highly flammable, and that is the major reason for its being discontinued. Surprisingly, many dolls have survived the ravages of time, but few are found in **MINT** condition.

The roses in the second row have a snake which jumps out when a bulb is pressed to send a surge of air into the flower. The roses are embossed "Made in Japan" on the petals, but the rubber bulbs are impressed MIOJ. Also in the second row is a rickshaw that white paint has been smeared over the wood impressed mark to make it stand out.

In the bottom row are two intriguing items. The second item is a stork and baby in a cage which attaches to the car window. No one had ever seen a Garfield stuck on the window in those days! The last item in the row is a baby rattle. I doubt that many of these survived!

Top Row:
    1st -7th, Football players, 6" (embossed on back) $ 7.50-10.00 ea.

Second Row:
    1st, Baby in crocheted dress (embossed on back)   35.00-45.00
    2nd-4th, Rose surprise (bulb impressed MIOJ)   4.00- 5.00 ea.
    5th-8th, Football players, 4" (cloverleaf emblem embossed)   5.00- 6.00 ea.
    9th, Rickshaw (impressed in wood)   10.00-12.50

Third Row:
    1st-12th, Zoo animals (embossed)   6.00- 8.00 ea.

Fourth Row:
    1st, Kewpie w/feathers (embossed on back)   22.50-25.00
    2nd, "Betty Boop," 8" (embossed leaf on back)   40.00-50.00
    3rd, "Betty Boop," 6" (embossed **S** in circle on back)   25.00-30.00
    4th, Baby, 11¾", moveable arms and legs (embossed on back)   60.00-75.00
    5th, Dutch girl, 8⅝" (embossed on back and has oriental symbol) 40.00-50.00
    6th, Kewpie, 6½" (embossed cloverleaf on back)   30.00-35.00

Fifth Row:
    1st, Black hula dancer w/bows (embossed on back)   30.00-35.00
    2nd, Stork in cage window bobber (stamped on bottom)   17.50-20.00
    3rd, Clown (Royal embossed Fleur de lis)   15.00-17.50
    4th, Baby (embossed on back)   12.50-15.00
    5th, Pink snow baby   15.00-17.50
    6th, Baby rattle (**5** in circle w/5 crosses)   20.00-22.50

CHICKENS, DUCKS and GEESE

Evidently, many feathered creatures were abundant on the Easter market in this time period. This was the time of dyed pink and blue live chickens and ducks as well. That is considered cruel to the animals today.

Actually the quality of some of the items photographed here is quite good. Some others are better looking in the photo than they really are.

The chicken pulling the cart in the bottom row has the MIOJ mark backwards. You have to hold it up to mirror to read it properly. Some collectors particularly enjoy oddities like that in their collections.

Top Row:
1st, Mallard planter (arch emblem)	$12.50-15.00
2nd, Duckling near hatched egg planter (arch emblem)	8.00-10.00
3rd, Duckling in egg planter (arch emblem)	8.00-10.00

Second Row:
1st, Rooster, two piece covered jar	25.00-35.00
2nd, Smaller rooster jar (**K** in circle)	20.00-25.00
3rd, Long-billed bird planter (blue)	5.00- 6.00

Third Row:
1st, Goose preening planter	4.00- 5.00
2nd, Chicken on basket	30.00-35.00
3rd, Mallard planter (arch emblem hand painted; brown)	12.50-15.00

Fourth Row:
1st, Small duck planter	4.00- 5.00
2nd, Blue and green duck planter (blue)	4.00- 5.00
3rd, Duck w/wings raised	10.00-12.50

Fifth Row:
1st, Goose planter (dark blue)	4.00- 5.00
2nd, Duck w/egg cart	12.50-15.00
3rd, Blue and green duck	8.00-10.00
4th, Chicken pulling cart (MIOJ mirror image)	6.00- 8.00

CHILDREN'S DISHES

Children's dishes are avidly collected whether they are Occupied Japan or not. The fact that some are marked Occupied Japan only adds to their collectibility because that means that more than one field of collectors is searching for the same pieces. Besides our field of collectors, doll collectors, collectors of children's dishes and even collectors of miniature items are all buying these pieces.

The "Doll's Nursing Set" in the top row is stamped on the box. This set has the bottle, a pacifier and even a rattle.

All the miniature tea sets shown in the second row have individual lids for the teapots and sugar bowls. The fourth small set w/roses even has the small cups marked on the bottom! (This set consists of coffee pot, four cup/saucer and the tray). Prices below are for complete sets with all lids.

* Set Prices

Two place setting consisting of: 2 cup & saucers, creamer, sugar w/lid, teapot w/lid (9 pieces)	$ 30.00- 35.00
Four place setting consisting of: 4 cup & saucers, creamer, sugar w/lid, teapot w/lid (13 pieces)	50.00- 55.00
Six place setting consisting of: 6 cup & saucers, creamer, sugar w/lid, 6 plates, teapot w/lid (23 pieces)	95.00-100.00
Six place setting w/serving pieces: same as above but adds covered casserole and platter (26 pieces)	115.00-125.00

* add $5.00 to 10.00 for box in good condition.

Top Row:

1st, Blue pottery-like creamer (red)	6.00- 8.00
2nd and 4th, Same cup and saucer	8.00- 10.00
4th, Floral luster creamer (red)	8.00- 10.00
5th, Same sugar w/lid	10.00- 12.50
6th, Doll's Nursing Set (box stamped)	40.00- 50.00

Second Row:

1st, Camel cup/saucer (red "Yamaga China")	10.00- 12.50
2nd, Miniature eight piece set (red)	8.00- 10.00
3rd, Miniature six piece set (red "Mariyama" set)	12.50- 15.00
4th, Miniature ten piece set ("Chubu China")	22.50- 25.00
5th, Blue Willow gravy and liner (blue)	35.00- 40.00

Third Row:

1st, Luster sugar (red)	6.00- 8.00
2nd and 3rd, Creamers (red)	6.00- 8.00 ea.
4th, Yellow floral four piece set (red)	50.00- 55.00

Fourth Row:

1st, Set, orange luster, two piece set in box (red)	30.00- 35.00
2nd, Set, Elephant set (red) plate	10.00- 12.00
Same cup and saucer	8.00- 10.00
Same sugar w/lid	10.00- 12.50
Same teapot w/lid	15.00- 17.50
Same creamer	8.00- 10.00
3rd, Miniature seven piece set w/wood display base	22.50- 25.00

Fifth Row:

1st, Seventeen piece set in box (red)	75.00- 90.00
2nd, Thirteen piece set in box (red)	55.00- 60.00

CHILDREN PAIRS and SINGLES

Finding children figurines in sets or pairs has become difficult in this collecting field. As with other Occupied Japan figurines, quality and size dictate prices. Notice that many toys and animals are also pictured with the children.

Some collectors only collect children with certain objects such as dogs or dolls. Finding children with dolls or toys seem to be the most difficult since other collectors besides us buy these depicted items. Some of the children pictured are similar to "Hummel" types, but most of these are only similar in style.

The white caped girl in the fourth row is normally found with a red cape and is usually sold as "Little Red Riding Hood." By the same token, the reclining boy w/horn in white on the bottom row is normally found in blue, and is usually sold as "Little Boy Blue."

Prices for individual figurines are half the lowest price of the pair!

Top Row:
1st, Flower girl, 4⅝ "	$10.00-12.50
2nd, Matching boy w/doll	12.50-15.00
3rd, Boy w/briefcase (red "Maruyama")	12.50-15.00
4th, Matching boy w/book	12.50-15.00
5th and 6th, Boy and girl (**T** thru **S** symbol)	25.00-30.00 pr.
7th and 8th, Girl w/rabbit and boy w/dog (red)	25.00-30.00 pr.

Second Row:
1st and 2nd, Girl and boy on fence 4"	27.50-30.00 pr.
3rd and 4th, Boy w/horn and girl w/satchel	22.50-25.00 pr.
5th and 6th, Boy w/toy horse and girl w/doll	30.00-35.00 pr.
7th, Boy w/book (red)	6.00- 8.00
8th, Boy w/umbrella (red)	6.00- 8.00

Third Row:
1st, Girl w/dog, 4⅛" (red)	8.00-10.00
2nd, Girl w/goose	6.00- 8.00
3rd, Boy w/duck and basket (red)	10.00-12.50
4th, Boy w/dog, 3" (red)	6.00- 8.00
5th, Boy w/dog, 4¼" (red)	10.00-12.50
6th, Boy w/rooster (red)	10.00-12.50
7th, Boy w/walking stick (red)	8.00-10.00
8th, Girl w/umbrella and dog (red)	8.00-10.00

Fourth Row:
1st, Girl w/"Betty Boop" doll, 3¾" (red cross in cloverleaf)	20.00-22.50
2nd, Girl w/duck	4.00- 5.00
3rd, Boy w/bird cage (red)	10.00-12.50
4th, Boy on fence w/bird (red)	5.00- 6.00
5th, Girl w/basket (red)	5.00- 6.00
6th, Girl on fence	5.00- 6.00
7th, "Little White Riding Hood," 4⅛" (red)	12.50-15.00
8th, Boy w/horn (red)	5.00- 6.00

Fifth Row:
1st, Girl in coat, 4⅛"	7.50-10.00
2nd and 3rd, Boys, 3¾"	8.00-10.00 ea.
4th, Girl w/scarf (red)	5.00- 6.00
5th, Seated girl w/book (red)	5.00- 6.00
6th, Seated girl w/book (red)	6.00- 8.00
7th, Reclining boy w/horn (blue)	7.50-10.00
8th, Nude w/wheat sheaf (red)	7.50-10.00

CHILDREN SINGLES

Many of these figurines may have mates or be parts of sets, but I have only found the ones shown. Finding mates to single figurines could become a full-time search, and I do not find enough time in my life to search singles haunts of the "Occupied Japan World."

Top Row:

1st, Boy w/saxophone, 4⅝"	$ 6.00- 8.00
2nd, Girl w/ teddy bear in basket, 5⅜" (red)	15.00-17.50
3rd and 4th, Goose girls (red)	10.00-12.50 ea.
5th, Girl w/lamb (red)	10.00-12.50
6th, Boy w/dog (red)	10.00-12.50
7th, Boy on fence w/basket (green)	8.00-10.00
8th, Blue boy (red)	6.00- 8.00

Second Row:

1st-4th, Skiers, 3½" (red)	10.00-12.50 ea.
5th and 6th, Skiers, 2⅛"	4.00- 5.00 ea.
7th and 8th, Girl w/flower or book	4.00- 5.00 ea.
9th, Boy on fence w/bird	5.00- 6.00
10th, Boy w/ bike	7.50-10.00

Third Row:

1st, Girl w/book/ basket, 3¾"	5.00- 6.00
2nd, Boy on fence w/basket, 4" (red)	6.00- 8.00
3rd, Boy w/satchel	6.00- 8.00
4th, Same as 2nd except 3½"	5.00- 6.00
5th, Boy w/blue bag	5.00- 6.00
6th, Boy walker (red)	5.00- 6.00
7th, Boy w/dog	2.00- 3.00
8th and 10th, Girl w/book or umbrella	5.00- 6.00 ea.
9th, Dutch boy (red)	6.00- 8.00

Fourth Row:

1st, Girl w/basket, 3⅛"	4.00- 5.00
2nd-4th, Girl w/duck and boys w/dog, 2¾"	2.50- 4.00 ea.
5th, Girl w/doll	4.00- 5.00
6th, Girl w/pitcher, 4" (red)	6.00- 8.00
7th, Girl w/curls	8.00-10.00
8th, Girl w/bucket	4.00- 5.00
9th, Boy w/dog and walking stick (red)	8.00-10.00
10th, Walking boy	10.00-12.50
11th, Boy w/dog, 2½" (red)	2.50- 4.00

Fifth Row:

1st, Girl w/doll buggy, 2½"	2.50- 4.00
2nd, Boy w/horn and 3rd, girl w/satchel	2.50- 4.00 ea.
4th, Boy w/truck	4.00- 5.00
5th-7th, Girls w/book or horn (red)	4.00- 5.00 ea.
8th, Girl w/chick and 9th, Boy w/pig	5.00- 6.00 ea.
10th and 11th, Boy w/dog, horn or on fence (red)	5.00- 6.00 ea.
12th and 13th, Girls on fence (red)	5.00- 6.00 ea.

CUP AND SAUCER SETS

The next four pictures show a wide selection of cup and saucers. Some are of excellent quality and others are poorly made as is the case of most items collected from Occupied Japan.

We have turned some of the cups and saucers to show their colorful interiors. Many of the sets shown in this section are ones that go with sets of dinnerware, so do not be surprised if you see a cup and saucer for which you are searching. Remember, all the pieces photographed in this book are sold in my shop, Grannie Bear Antiques if you spot a set you need. Maybe it will still be in our inventory!

Top Row:

1st, Set, "Trimont China," pink w/flower	$17.50-20.00
2nd, Set, "Diamond China"	8.00-10.00
3rd, Set (Horse w/knight)	15.00-17.50

Second Row:

1st, Set, "Lenwile China," HP, "Ardalt 6194"	20.00-22.50
2nd, Set, yellow floral (gray)	10.00-12.50
3rd, Set, "Diamond China," black w/gold netting floral	15.00-17.50

Third Row:

1st, Set, blue rim floral (blue **M.B.**)	8.00-10.00
2nd, Set, red rim floral	8.00-10.00
3rd, Set, "Ucagco China," w/emblem (gold)	10.00-12.50
4th, Set, "luster," w/house scene (red)	10.00-12.50

Fourth Row:

1st, Set, gold rimmed floral (red)	8.00-10.00
2nd, Set, (red **G M C**) w/fancy **M**	8.00-10.00
3rd, Set, "luster" w/pagoda scene (red)	10.00-12.50
4th, Set, "luster" rim w/floral (elephant head over **A** emblem)	8.00-10.00

Fifth Row:

1st, Set, "Diamond China," blue w/floral	10.00-12.50
2nd, Set, "Diamond China," (**LEDA** in gold on side)	15.00-17.50
3rd, Set, "Diamond China," white floral	10.00-12.50
4th, Set, floral w/fancy handle (red)	12.50-15.00

CUP and SAUCER SETS (Cont.)

As shown on the previous page, the top rows have been set up to show both saucers and the inside of the cup. Also, there are a couple of sets which have a mark of a knight on horseback along with the Occupied Japan.

The blue and white set shown in the second row almost fits the "flow blue" category. The design contains people, horses and a house. This set along with several others on this page may be found in complete dinnerware sets.

The most recognizable set in this picture is the "Phoenix Bird" pattern shown as the first set on the fourth row. This is a highly collected pattern whether it is marked Occupied Japan or not. Most "Phoenix Bird" collectors make little distinction as to the mark!

Top Row:
1st, Set, black floral (red Merit in wreath)	$15.00-17.50
2nd, Set, "Trimont China HP", orange rim, floral	17.50-20.00
3rd, Set, black floral (knight on horse, "exclusively MIOJ," **G.Z.L.**, U.S.A.)	15.00-17.50

Second Row:
1st, Set, "Vartix Earthenware Superfine", blue and white (blue)	22.50-25.00
2nd, Set, "Orion China HP," floral (red)	10.00-12.50
3rd, Set, black floral (knight on horse, "exclusively MIOJ")	15.00-17.50

Third Row:
1st, Set, floral (red)	8.00-10.00
2nd, Set, "Ucagco China" w/emblem (gold)	10.00-12.50
3rd Set, floral w/blue "luster" rim (red **K A** in diamond)	8.00-10.00
4th Set, floral (red Merit in wreath)	10.00-12.50

Fourth Row:
1st, Set "Phoenix Bird" (blue)	22.50-25.00
2nd, Set, "Diamond China", rust rimmed, floral	8.00-10.00
3rd, Set, floral w/stripe (red)	6.00- 8.00
4th, Set, floral w/blue "luster" rim (red)	8.00-10.00

Fifth Row:
1st, Set, "Aladdin Fine China," HOLLANDIA, tulip design	10.00-12.50
2nd, Set, "Trimont China," pink rimmed	8.00-10.00
3rd, Set, "Merit China HP," floral ribbed (red)	15.00-17.50
4th, Set, "Merit China," blue rimmed, floral interior	10.00-12.50

CUP and SAUCER SETS (Cont.)

It has been unusual to find more than two or three matching cup and saucers sporting different colors. Take note of the six matching sets in the third and fourth rows. I say six because the black and white cup in the third row is not marked "Ardalt" as are the others even though it matches them in every other way. Evidently this was a popular mould for "Ardalt" or there was some sort of demitasse set with mixed colors. All demitasse sets I have seen before have had matching colors, however; so this may not be the case. No matter, they make a wonderful set to search for in your travels. Maybe there are other colors!

Shown on the fourth row is a demitasse cup and saucer in the "Phoenix Bird" pattern. This size cup seems to be harder to find than the standard size coffee or tea cup "Occupied Japan" markings.

The third cup in the bottom row is one of the pieces pictured alone in the book that is not marked "Occupied Japan." It should not be here. This cup was bought with a large Occupied Japan collection, and the marking (Bavarian, Schumann, Germany, U.S. Zone) was not noticed until after photographing. Since it slipped in, it seemed easier to leave than to redo the whole page. It does give me the chance to comment that you will often find pieces in a set of Occupied Japan that are only marked Japan. In a set of china the plates may be marked MIOJ and some other pieces may not be. They can only be considered OJ if they remain with the set. Oft times **both** cup and saucer are not marked. You should have seen the tables and boxes of Occupied Japan at this photography session. It took over five days to photograph!

Top Row:
1st, Set, "Tamaka," floral demi (red)	$ 8.00-10.00
2nd, Set, "Violet China," white floral demi (blue)	8.00-10.00
3rd, Set, "Paulux," rose on tri-footed cup (gold)	15.00-17.50
4th, Set, "Jyoto China," white floral (gold)	8.00-10.00
5th, Set, "Cherry China," white floral (blue)	8.00-10.00

Second Row:
1st, Set, rust floral, "Hadson" (red anchor mark)	10.00-12.50
2nd, Set, "Berkshire Fine China," blue floral rim (gold)	8.00-10.00
3rd, Set, "Merit China," green floral rim (red)	10.00-12.50
4th, Set, footed, black w/gold (blue)	17.50-20.00

Third Row:
1st, Demi set, black and white w/gold design (red)	15.00-17.50
2nd-5th, Sets, same as above only marked "No 6120 Ardalt" H.P. (red)	15.00-17.50 ea.

Fourth Row:
1st, Set, "Phoenix Bird," demi (blue)	22.50-25.00
2nd, Set, "Chugai China," yellow interior (gold mountain symbol)	12.50-15.00
3rd, Set, white demi floral w/saucer marked w/clover in wreath	6.00- 8.00
4th and 5th, Sets, marked as in third row	12.50-15.00 ea.

Fifth Row:
1st, Set, dark green swirl demi (gold)	22.50-25.00
2nd, Set, "Jyoto China," yellow demi (gold)	10.00-12.50
3rd, Set, (See last paragraph above)	5.00- 6.00
4th, Set, "Royal Sealy" (gold; mountain in wreath)	12.50-15.00
5th, Set, white floral swirled design (gray; circle w/rectangle)	12.50-15.00

CUP and SAUCER SETS (Cont.)

I have shown odd cups before, but these odd saucers are too colorful to omit. Prices for saucers are usually reasonable unless you order from a "matching service." Oft times that may be the only place where pieces to "named" sets can be found. Finding pieces to match sets that are not named on the back or shown in a book can be a trying experience!

Top Row:
1st, Saucer, "Trimont China," gray w/pink flower (gold)	$ 2.00- 3.00
2nd, Saucer, "Merit," black w/pink flower (red)	2.00- 3.00
3rd, Saucer, "Trimont China," black w/pink flower (gold)	2.00- 3.00
4th, Saucer, "Diamond China," black acorn w/white oak leaf (?)	2.00- 3.00

Second Row:
1st, Saucer, "Mocco," yellow rimmed (blue)	1.50- 2.00
2nd, Saucer, blue w/pink flower (red; large **M** over **B**)	2.00- 3.00
3rd, Saucer, "Merit," yellow w/floral (gold)	2.00- 3.00
4th, Saucer, "Waco China," royal red w/flower	2.00- 3.00

Third Row:
1st, Set, "Gold China," swirled white w/flower	6.00- 8.00
2nd, Set, brown rim w/floral (red)	5.00- 6.00
3rd, Set, demi set floral (red; elephant over **A**)	5.00- 6.00
4th, Set, demi "luster" w/floral (green)	5.00- 6.00
5th, Set, demi six-sided black/red/white (red)	10.00-12.50

Fourth Row:
1st, Set, demi black floral (red)	6.00- 8.00
2nd, Set, pagoda scene (red)	7.50-10.00
3rd, Set, green w/gold decoration (red)	7.50-10.00
4th, Set, white w/gold souvenir Fayetteville, N.C.	5.00- 6.00
5th, Set, pink floral (red)	4.00- 5.00
6th, Set, blue w/scalloped rim (red)	5.00- 6.00

Fifth Row:
1st, St. Denis, size 3" floral ("Hadson" inverted horseshoe type mark)	10.00-12.50
2nd, St. Denis, size basket, decorated (red)	8.00-10.00
3rd, Set, "Mother," 4⅛" (**S.G.A.** basket in wreath emblem)	22.50-25.00
4th, Cup, "Mother," decorated floral (red)	17.50-20.00

DECORATIVE ITEMS – CHRISTMAS, CLOCKS and COACHES

Christmas collectibles are gaining in popularity and that makes our Occupied Japan ones even more difficult to obtain. Several books on Christmas items have been released in recent years and that makes more knowledgeable collectors. Several of these books have priced Occupied Japan items "out of sight" compared to prices that had previously been paid. This is another problem for those of us who have collected for many years. Collectors of other collecting fraternities raise our prices by paying more than we have been used to paying. As Occupied Japan collectors we will have to adjust our buying habits or be left without any of these type pieces to purchase.

The papier mache Santas are purchased as soon as they come on the market. Most of these are found with paper labels; so if they were ever used, the labels are usually long gone. Other times the Santas are marked with what appears to be a rubber stamp.

Shown here are a dozen different "Occupied Japan" clocks. Doll and miniature collectors are rapidly drying this field up also. Doll collectors use these small clocks in doll houses.

The last two items in the bottom row are Souvenir items issued by an "Occupied Japan" Collectors Club in California. One is a pin and the other is a mug. The mug is dated 1982 and is one of 300. It is also signed by R. W. Lee, President and founder. Yes, it has now become collectible!

Top Row:
    1st, Cuckoo clock, 5" w/pendulums on string (red) $12.50-15.00
    2nd, Christmas bulb tree, paper label   8.00-10.00
    3rd, Bulbs, "fancy class ball Ornament Doz. Maker
        OHN 32/1477   25.00-30.00
    4th, Santa, red papier mache (stamped on bottom)   40.00-50.00
    5th, Santa, blue w/silver hat (paper label)   40.00-50.00

Second Row:
    1st-4th, Tree ornaments (paper label)   10.00-12.50 ea.

Third Row:
    1st, Clock, 2", "Souvenir of Bely Clocks" (red)   6.00- 8.00
    2nd-5th, Clocks 3¾" several styles (red)   8.00-10.00 ea.

Fourth Row:
    1st, Child house (red)   4.00- 5.00
    2nd, 3rd and 5th, Clocks (red)   6.00- 8.00 ea.
    4th, Clock w/dog (red)   8.00-10.00
    6th, Cuckoo w/pendulums on string   8.00-10.00

Fifth Row:
    1st, Coach, 3" high (red)   8.00-10.00
    2nd and 3rd, Coaches, 2½" high (red)   6.00- 8.00 ea.
    4th, Occupied Japan Club pin   12.50-15.00
    5th, Occupied Japan Collector's Club mug   20.00-25.00

DECORATIVE ITEMS – PLATES and BOWLS

There are many decorative "Occupied Japan" plates that would sell for double the price (or more) if they were marked "Germany," "Austrian" or even "Bavarian." Quality workmanship is sometimes disdained because it says Japanese in some form. Oddly enough, collectors do not attach the same stigma to "Nippon" which means the same thing. "Nippon" marked items only have an age factor of at least fifteen years earlier than Occupied Japan.

For years I have heard that many pieces of Occupied Japan were actually European made, but marked "Occupied Japan" to save import duties. No one has ever proved that fact to me. Old time "antique dealers" were the first people to tell me those stories, but I suspected they justified selling quality pieces of MIOJ that way. In any case some of the lattice ware decorated plates rival any thing that ever came out of Europe.

Another problem you may run into is MIOJ marks scratched off the back of these plates. I recently ran into one of these at an Antique Mall in Tennessee. I have never heard of any one removing a European mark; but old fashioned dealers still feel MIOJ merchandise is beneath the dignity of their shops. Thus they "remove" or at least, used to "remove" the now valuable MIOJ mark!

Top Row:
1st, Plate, 7", ("Gold China"), signed "Ito" in purple on front	$25.00-35.00
2nd, Plate, 6" open ribbon plate ("Ucagco China" w/emblem in gold)	20.00-22.50
3rd, Lattice plate, 6" ("Rosetti" Chicago, U.S.A., HP in brown)	22.50-25.00
4th, Fruit plate, signed "Parry" on front ("Celebrate" in gold)	20.00-22.50

Second Row:
1st, Two leaves candy or relish, 5½" long (red)	6.00- 8.00
2nd, Handled plate, 4¼" (HP green)	8.00-10.00
3rd, Handled plate, 4¼" (red)	8.00-10.00
4th and 5th, Floral plates, 4½" ("Aiyo China" in red)	8.00-10.00 ea.

Third Row:
1st-3rd, Floral bowls, 5½" (red **G** in wreath)	10.00-12.50 ea.
4th, Lattice edge floral plate ("Rosetti" Chicago, U.S.A., HP in red)	10.00-12.50
5th, Lattice edge fruit bowl, 5½" (red)	15.00-17.50

Fourth Row:
1st, Brown tri-plate w/floral (embossed)	10.00-12.50
2nd, Brown leaf-shaped plate (embossed)	8.00-10.00
3rd, Brown floral plate (embossed)	4.00- 5.00
4th, Brown bowl (yellow **M** over top **G**)	4.00- 5.00
5th, Brown cloverleaf shape plate (embossed)	8.00-10.00

DECORATIVE ITEMS - PLATES and BOWLS (Cont.)

Many of the smaller plates were souvenir items and can be found with the original prices of 19 or 29 cents in black crayon on the back.

The top row has three fruit plates. The first is either blackberries or black raspberries. The second is red raspberries and the third is anyone's guess. Maybe they are gooseberries, but I suspect that they are some type of fruit indigenous to Japan rather than the United States.

In the third row is a plate translated as "It's later than you think." If any reader can translate the Japanese above that line, let me know if that is what it really says.

Top Row:

1st, Small leaf, 2½" (blue)	$ 2.00- 3.00
2nd-4th, Fruit plates, 6" ("Ohata China"; green)	12.50-15.00 ea.
5th, Small leaf, 2½"	2.00- 3.00

Second Row:

1st, Palette signed "V. Soga" ("Ardalt" HP in red)	12.50-15.00
2nd, Palette signed "K. Ohi"	10.00-12.50
3rd, Oval, 7½" lattice edged bowl ("Aiyo China" HP; red)	20.00-22.50
4th, Bowl, 4½" lattice edge bowl ("Gold China"; purple)	12.50-15.00

Third Row:

1st, Maple leaf (red)	2.00- 3.00
2nd, Dog plate, 2¾" (green)	6.00- 8.00
3rd and 5th, Small flower plate	2.00- 3.00 ea.
4th, Leaf w/bee (red)	4.00- 5.00
6th, Tray w/translation (red HP)	4.00- 5.00
7th, Embossed rose on tray (red)	4.00- 5.00

Fourth Row:

1st, Fish on shell-shaped tray signed "Burge Puemaii" (red)	6.00- 8.00
2nd and 5th, Scenic plates (red)	2.50- 4.00 ea.
3rd and 4th, Scenic plates ("Ucagco China" w/emblem; gold)	4.00- 5.00 ea.
6th, Clover scene ("Chugai China" mountain symbol; gold)	8.00-10.00
7th, Sea shell, 3" w/violets (red)	2.50- 4.00

Fifth Row:

1st, Handled floral bowl (red HP)	10.00-12.50
2nd, Sea shell, 4" (red **M** in wreath)	4.00- 5.00
3rd, Handled "luster" bowl (red)	7.50-10.00
4th, Handled plate, 4¼" (crown symbol "Rosetti" Chicago U.S.A. HP in red)	6.00- 8.00
5th, Handled plate, 4¼" (crown symbol "Rosetti" Chicago U.S.A. HP in green)	6.00- 8.00

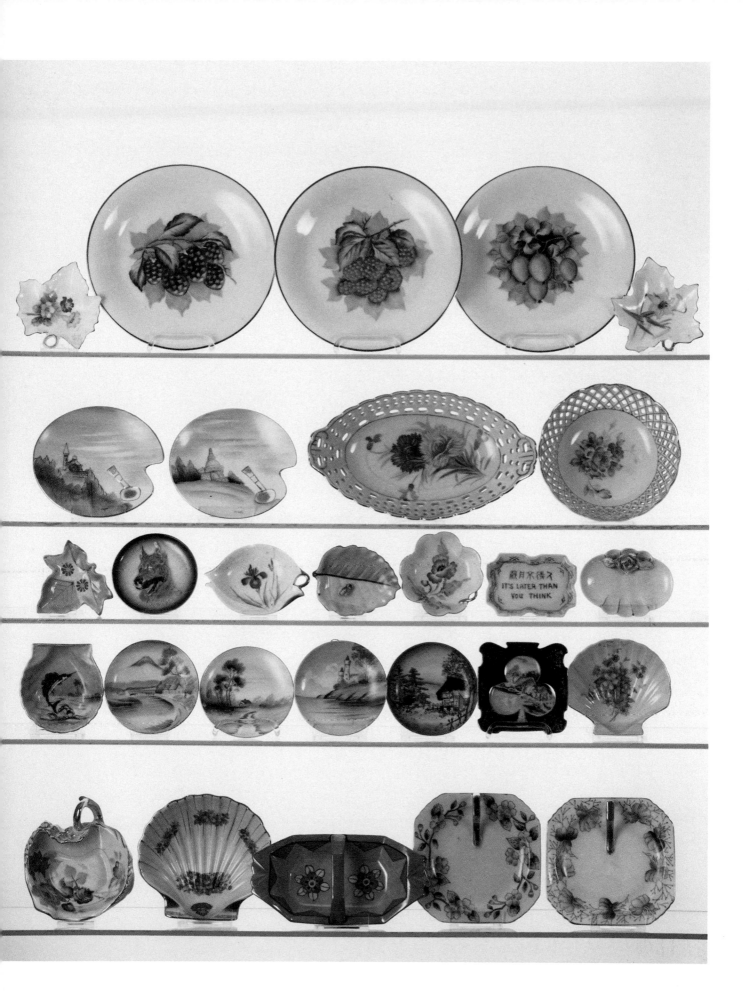

DINNERWARE

The following five pages show many examples of "Occupied Japan" dinnerware. I will list the names of each known pattern and list some guidelines for prices. Each pattern will be designated as an "**A**" or "**B**" pattern. Prices for patterns listed as "**A**" will be the higher prices below, and "**B**" pattern prices the lower.

Amazingly, whole Occupied Japan dinnerware sets do not sell easily! People, in general, do not buy sets for which they cannot find replacements, or at least that has been my experience with Occupied Japan dinnerware. Individual pieces are also hard to sell unless someone is looking for that particular pattern. In that event, you will pay a premium to get cups, dinner plates and serving pieces which were not sold with all sets. Therefore, if you add up the cost of individual pieces, you will find that the parts are more costly than if the whole set were bought at once.

Set prices are below and individual prices are on page 54.

Realize that most patterns are unnamed and that is why I am including as many examples as I can. If I can show a pattern you collect, then you have a reference point to show to someone helping you look for your pattern.

Page 49 (**A**) "Sango China" floral pattern w/floral rim

Page 50 (**A**) "Diamond China" floral pattern w/rust colored rim (comes w/other colored rims)
Page 51 (**A**) "Aladdin Fine China" GARLAND pattern w/aladdin lamp emblem

Page 52 (**A**) Top row (1st-3rd), "Ucagco China" w/emblem in gold (yellow flower pattern)
           (**B**) 4th, "Regal China" EMERALD pattern w/crown emblem
           (**B**) 5th, "Yamaka China" (bamboo-like pattern)
           (**A**) Second row left, "Noritake China"
           (**A**) Second row right, "Norumi China" MAGNOLIA pattern
           (**A**) Third row left, "Noritake China" **M** in wreath mark
           (**B**) Third row right, (red mark) (gold swirl on white pattern)

Page 53 (**A**) Top row left, "Rosetti" SPRING VIOLETS gold mark crown
           (**B**) Top row right, "Hadson Chinaware" red anchor mark (ivy type pattern)
           (**A**) Second row, "Gold" Hand Painted (floral pattern)
           (**B**) Third row, "Hadson Chinaware" red anchor mark (yellow rose pattern)

Set for four including: cups, saucers, plates in 3 sizes, berry and soup bowls creamer and covered sugar	175.00-200.00
Set for 6 including all of above and cereal bowls, gravy boat and small platter	225.00-250.00
Set for 8 including all of above and 2 platters	275.00-300.00
Set for 12 including all of above and adding covered casserole and turkey platter	400.00-450.00

DINNERWARE (Cont.)

The most widely known Japanese dinnerware pattern is "Blue Willow." More than one company made this pattern and the quality varies greatly. Some pieces are heavily crazed and stain easily, while others look as good today as when first made.

Prices for the "Blue Willow" pictured on page 51 are listed here. I will not attempt to price anything that is not shown. All the other items priced individually are from dinnerware sets pictured on pages 45-49.

All items marked "Kakusa China" in top two rows

Top Row:

1st, Cereal bowl, 5¾"	$12.50-15.00
2nd, Sugar w/lid	17.50-20.00
3rd, Creamer	12.50-15.00
4th, Berry bowl, 4¾"	10.00-12.50

Second Row:

1st, Cup and saucer	17.50-20.00
2nd, Salad plate, 7"	6.00- 8.00
3rd, Dinner plate, 9"	12.50-15.00

Third Row:

1st, Demitasse cup and saucer, "Ironstone Ware" (green)	17.50-20.00
2nd, Cup and saucer, same as 1st	15.00-17.50
3rd, Demitasse saucer, "Maryta China" in wreath-like emblem	4.00- 5.00
4th, Cup and saucer, same as 3rd	17.50-20.00

Individual Pieces Of Dinnerware (pages 45-49)

Ash tray (few patterns)	2.50- 4.00
Bowl, berry (4" to 4⅞")	4.00- 5.00
Bowl, cereal (5" to 6½")	6.00- 8.00
Bowl, soup (7" to 9")	8.00-10.00
Bowl, round vegetable (9½" to 10½")	22.50-25.00
Bowl, oval vegetable (10" to 12")	25.00-30.00
Casserole, covered	35.00-45.00
Comport or compote (few patterns)	20.00-22.50
Creamer	12.50-15.00
Cup	8.00-15.00
Gravy	12.50-15.00
Gravy platter	8.00-10.00
Gravy w/attached platter	25.00-30.00
Plate, bread and butter (5¾" to 6¾")	2.50- 4.00
Plate, salad (7" to 8")	5.00- 6.00
Plate, dinner (9" to 11")	10.00-15.00
Platter, small oval (9½" to 11")	12.50-15.00
Platter, medium oval (12" to 15")	22.50-25.00
Platter, large turkey (16" to 19"	40.00-75.00
Saucer	1.00- 3.00
Sugar w/cover	15.00-20.00

ETHNIC REPRESENTATIVES

The ethnic cultures represented by the figurines of this time period were multitudinous. Black and American Indian figurines are collected by many. Most of these were made in stereotypes; so many have been broken over the years. I personally know of some black people who used to make it their mission in life to remove as many stereotype personifications from the market as possible.

The pie bird on the end of the top row is an expensive piece of culture. You can also find this "Mammy" unmarked, but this is marked "Occupied Japan" in red. I have two different collectors who want to buy this one when I am finished with it. One collects pie birds and has never seen one marked "Occupied Japan!"

In the third row, the hula dancer is marked "SAMPLE." This is not unusual as I have seen at least fifty pieces so marked over the years. Next to hula dancer is an Indian pencil sharpener. Many pencil sharpeners of this time period are Occupied Japan, but few people ever find the mark without some searching.

Cathy, my wife, collects Dutch related items and the fourth and part of the fifth row are from her collection.

Top Row:

1st and 2nd, Aborigine pair, 4¾" (red)	$ 40.00-50.00
3rd, Snake charmer couple vase, 5½"	20.00-22.50
4th, Black fiddling boy	20.00-22.50
5th, Indian winding turban, 6"	17.50-20.00
6th, "Mammy" pie bird (red)	75.00-100.00

Second Row:

1st, Boy w/fiddle, 3" (red)	15.00-17.50
2nd, Boy w/horn, 3" (red)	15.00-17.50
3rd, Gray faced fiddler (red)	12.50-15.00
4th, Cowboy on horse (red)	10.00-12.50
5th, Cowboy vase (red)	10.00-12.50
6th, Indian girl bud vase, 3⅝"	8.00-10.00
7th, Indian chief bud vase, 3⅝" (red)	8.00-10.00

Third Row:

1st and 2nd, Dutch pair w/detachable buckets, 4¼" (blue)	15.00-17.50 ea.
3rd, Hula girl w/grass skirt	7.50-10.00
4th, Hula girl (marked "sample" in red)	10.00-12.50
5th, Indian head metal pencil sharpener (embossed)	12.50-15.00
6th, Ash tray metal, "Howdy Podner" (embossed)	4.00- 5.00
7th, Indian head (Souvenir of White Pine Lodge, Deerwood, Minn.)	12.50-15.00

Fourth Row:

1st, Dutch girl, 3¼"	5.00- 6.00
2nd, Dutch girl shaker (red)	6.00- 8.00
3rd, Dutch boy bust shaker (red)	6.00- 8.00
4th, Dutch boy w/pipe (match to 1st)	5.00- 6.00
5th, Dutch girl w/basket, 4½" (red)	12.50-15.00
6th, Dutch girl w/basket, 3⅛"	8.00-10.00
7th, Dutch girl seated shaker	6.00- 8.00
8th, Dutch boy w/buckets (red)	8.00-10.00

Fifth Row:

1st, Girl with bowl on head, 4½" (red)	6.00- 8.00
2nd, Girl w/ bowl on head and vase, 5" (red)	7.50-10.00
3rd, Cowboy, 5⅛"	8.00-10.00
4th and 5th, Dutch couple, 6⅛" (red)	15.00-17.50 ea.
6th and 7th, Snake charming, pr. (red)	20.00-22.50 pr.

FIGURINE PAIRS

The next three photos all show matched pairs in varying degrees of quality. Prices indicate those of exceptiona
workmanship. Any figurines **over 8"** are hard to find!

Remember that individual figurines are half the lowest price of the pair!

Page 59

Top Row:

1st, Couple, 7¼" lady w/duck and basket; man w/rabbit (red)	$30.00-40.00
2nd, Couple, 6½" seated "Maruyama" (red)	85.00-95.00
3rd, Couple, 7½", lady w/hat; man w/cloak and hat	30.00-35.00

Second Row:

1st, Couple, 5", open holed figurines (red)	20.00-22.50
2nd, Couple w/dogs, 5½" (red)	20.00-25.00
3rd, Couple w/arms up and dogs	35.00-40.00

Second Row: (Cont.)

4th, Dutch people at well	22.50-25.00

Third Row:

1st, Colonial couple, 10⅛", "Orion China"	65.00-85.00
2nd, Couple, 10" (red)	50.00-60.00

Fourth Row:

1st, Couple w/hats, 6½"	30.00-40.00
2nd, Couple w/mandolin and book "Maruyama"	65.00-85.00
3rd, Couple white w/gold, 6½"	30.00-40.00

Page 60

Top Row:

1st, Couple, 6⅛" cloaks & mandolin	$30.00-40.00
2nd, Couple, 6" decorated Delft (red)	40.00-55.00
3rd, Couple, 7" man w/stick and woman w/umbrella (red)	25.00-30.00
4th, Couple w/flowers, 5¼" (red H.P.)	22.50-25.00

Second Row:

1st, Couple, 5¼" pink on Delft	30.00-35.00
2nd, Couple, 4⅝" (red)	12.50-15.00
3rd, Couple (red)	15.00-17.50
4th, Dutch couple, 4⅛" (red)	15.00-17.50
5th, Colonial couple (red mark on girl)	8.00-10.00
6th, Couple in white	8.00-10.00

Third Row:

1st, Couple, 7½" (red basket emblem)	30.00-35.00
2nd, Colonial couple, 7¼" (red)	40.00-50.00
3rd, Couple w/green hats, 8⅛" (red)	60.00-75.00
4th, Couple, 7" (blue)	30.00-35.00

Fourth Row:

1st, Couple white w/gold, 6⅛" (red anchor mark)	35.00-40.00
2nd, Hatted couple (red)	20.00-22.50
3rd, Musical couple (red **L.D.** face mark)	35.00-45.00
4th, Couple white w/gold, 6⅜" (red)	35.00-40.00

Page 61

Top Row:

1st, Colonial couple, 5⅝" (red)	$25.00-30.00
2nd, Colonial couple, 8¹/₁₆" (red)	50.00-65.00
3rd, Couple, 7" buxom lady; man w/flower (red)	40.00-50.00

Second Row:

1st, Couple, 4⅛" (red)	12.50-15.00
2nd, Couple w/flowers	12.50-15.00
3rd, Couple in fancy dress (red)	15.00-17.50
4th, Blue couple (red)	15.00-17.50

Third Row:

1st and 2nd, Pastoral and Dutch couples, 5" (red)	12.50-15.00 pr.

Third Row: (Cont.)

3rd, Couple	12.50-15.00
4th, Colonial couple (red)	17.50-20.00

Fourth Row:

1st, Pastel couple, 5"	15.00-17.50
2nd and 3rd, Couples (red)	12.50-15.00
4th, Couple, 4" (red)	7.50-10.00

Fifth Row:

1st, Musical couple, 4⅝"	15.00-17.50
2nd, Seated musicians, 4⅛"	15.00-17.50
3rd, Same as 2nd only 3½"	10.00-12.50
4th, Seated, 3" pin cushion musicians	20.00-25.00

FIGURINES - ORIENTALS

The next three pictures show a wide variety of Oriental figurines. Pages 63 and 64 show pairs or sets and Page 65 shows single figurines.

Remember that individual figurines are half the lowest price of the pair!

Page 63

Top Row:

1st, Couple, 4" musicians	$10.00-12.50
2nd, Couple, 4⅞"	12.50-15.00
3rd, Couple, 5⅜" (red)	17.50-20.00
4th, Bisque se,t 4⅝"	10.00-12.50 ea.

Second Row:

1st, Seated pair, 2¾" (blue)	20.00-25.00
2nd and 3rd, Old and young	12.50-15.00 pr.
4th, Couple, 3⅛" (red)	7.50-10.00
5th, Boy and girl, 4⅝" (red)	12.50-15.00

Third Row:

1st, Couple, 8¼" girl w/fan; man w/dagger (red)	25.00-35.00

Third Row: (Cont.)

2nd, Dancers, 7½" (blue **R** in shield)	60.00-75.00
3rd, Couple, 7" girl (red)	30.00-40.00

Fourth Row:

1st-5th, Set, 7½" "Moriyama" basket of flowers emblem	17.50-20.00 set
6th-9th, Set, "Ucagco China" w/emblem in red	15.00-17.50 set

Page 64

Top Row:

1st and 3rd, Couples, 6½" (red)	$17.50-20.00 pr.
2nd, Couple, 4" (red)	8.00-10.00
4th, Couple w/ pig, "Ucagco China" w/emblem and duck (OJ)	17.50-20.00
5th, Couple, 4" girl souvenir of Boston Mass.	12.50-15.00

Second Row:

1st, Kissing couple, "Rosetti, Chicago, U.S.A." in blue	30.00-32.50
2nd and 3rd, Same as 1st but only marked in red	30.00-32.50 pr.

Third Row:

1st and 2nd, Couples, 8¼" (red)	50.00-65.00 pr.
3rd, Skinny yellow couple, 7¼"	22.50-25.00

Fourth Row:

1st, Similar to Page 59, Row 3, Only both (red)	30.00-40.00
2nd, Older couple (red)	30.00-35.00
3rd, Children, 7½" (red)	35.00-45.00
4th, Couple w/black pants, 6⅛"	25.00-30.00

Page 65

Top Row:

1st, Singing boy, 5½"	$10.00-12.50
2nd, Man w/hat	12.50-15.00
3rd and 5th, Lady w/fan and man w/mandolin (red)	10.00-12.50 ea.
4th, Warrior on horse, 6½" (red H.P.)	20.00-22.50
6th, Lady (red)	6.00- 8.00
7th, Boy w/basket	12.50-15.00

Second Row:

1st, Warrior, 3¾" (red)	6.00- 8.00
2nd, Bearded man (red)	7.50-10.00
3rd and 7th-9th, Musicians (red)	10.00-12.50 ea.
4th and 5th, Boys (red)	6.00- 8.00 ea.
6th, Lady w/child (red H.P.)	17.50-20.00

Third Row:

1st, Girl, 5¾" w/folded hands	8.00-10.00
2nd and 5th, Man w/beard or flute	10.00-12.50 ea.
3rd, Girl with basket, 8"	15.00-17.50
4th and 7th, Man and woman (red)	12.50-15.00 ea.
6th, Musician w/foot up, 6¼"	12.50-15.00
8th, Seated boy	6.00- 8.00

Fourth Row:

1st, Warrior, 4⅛" (red)	7.50-10.00
2nd and 3rd, Girl or boy	8.00-10.00 ea
4th, Rickshaw (red)	15.00-17.50
5th, Oriental cowboy (red)	12.50-15.00
6th, Couple (red)	7.50-10.00
7th, Boy, 7⅞"	20.00-22.50
8th, Dancer (red)	12.50-15.00

FIGURINES - SINGLES and SEATED COUPLES

I have used this "singles" term to indicate figurines for which I have found no matching partner. I feel confident that most, if not all, should have a mate out there somewhere.

Page 67

Top Row:

1st, Lady w/basket, 5¾" (red)	$ 8.00-10.00
2nd and 6th, Lady w/fan or basket	10.00-12.50 ea.
3rd, Lady w/purple skirt	12.50-15.00
4th, Brown/white lady, 8¼" (red)	30.00-40.00
5th, Lady lifting skirt (red)	15.00-17.50
7th, Peasant lady (red)	10.00-12.50

Second Row:

1st, Lady w/mandolin, 4" (brown)	5.00- 6.00
2nd, 4th and 5th, Ladies (red)	7.50-10.00 ea.
3rd, Gent, 3¾" (red)	2.50- 4.00
6th,8th and 9th, Ladies (red)	4.00- 5.00 ea.
7th, Lady w/basket, 5⅜"	10.00-12.50
10th, Lady **K.I.** in emblem	4.00- 5.00

Third Row:

1st, Lady w/red shawl, 3½" (red)	4.00- 5.00
2nd-4th, Ladies w/dog or deer, 4½" (red)	15.00-17.50 ea.
5th and 8th, Ladies, 5" (red)	12.50-15.00 ea.
6th and 7th, Ladies (red)	6.00- 8.00 ea.

Fourth Row:

1st and 6th, Ladies, 7⅛" (red)	15.00-17.50 ea.
2nd, Well endowed lady, 8" (red)	30.00-35.00
3rd, Lady w/ feathers in hair, 10⅜" (red)	55.00-75.00
4th, Buxom lady, 10" (red)	55.00-75.00
5th, Peasant lady, 8"	25.00-30.00

Page 68

Top Row:

1st, Seated man, 4½" (red)	$10.00-12.50
2nd and 5th, Seated ladies, 5⅛" (red)	12.50-15.00 ea.
3rd and 4th, Lady planters, 6⅜" (red)	15.00-17.50 ea.
6th, Couple on bench	8.00-10.00
7th, Couple on couch, 4" high (red)	17.50-20.00

Second Row:

1st, 2nd and 6th, Seated, 3" (red)	5.00- 6.00 ea.
3rd, Children on couch (red)	17.50-20.00
4th, Seated lady	4.00- 5.00
5th, Seated man, "Maruyama" in red	10.00-12.50
7th,9th and 10th, Seated figures, 2¾" (red)	2.50- 4.00 ea.
8th, Seated couple	15.00-17.50

Third Row:

1st and 2nd, Couple, 3" seated (red)	10.00-12.50 pr.

Third Row: (Cont.)

3rd and 4th, Couple (red H.P.)	6.00- 8.00 pr.
5th and 6th, Couple (red)	10.00-12.50 pr.
7th-9th, Ladies (red)	7.50-10.00 ea.

Fourth Row:

1st, Lady w/living bra, 4½"	5.00- 6.00
2nd-4th, Men (red)	2.50- 4.00 ea.
5th, Lady w/dog	15.00-17.50
6th,8th and 9th, Ladies (red)	6.00- 8.00 ea.
7th, Lady (red H.P.)	8.00-10.00

Fifth Row:

1st, Lady, 4" (blue)	6.00- 8.00
2nd,3rd, 9th-11th, Figures (red)	6.00- 8.00 ea.
4th and 7th, Lady and man (red)	2.50- 4.00 ea.
5th and 6th, Seated ladies	4.00- 5.00 ea.
8th Lady (red)	7.50-10.00

Page 69

Top Row:

1st, Man w/blue coat, 6"	$10.00-12.50
2nd, 4th and 5th, Men	10.00-12.50 ea.
3rd, Man "Ucagco China" w/emblem in red	12.50-15.00
6th, Mandolin player	17.50-20.00
7th and 8th, Men (red)	10.00-12.50 ea.

Second Row:

1st, Balloon man, 3½"	12.50-15.00
2nd and 3rd, Men	6.00-8.00 ea.
4th-8th, Men (red or black)	4.00-5.00 ea.
9th and 10th, Men (red)	7.50-10.00 ea.

Third Row:

1st-3rd, Men, 4⅛"	4.00-5.00 ea.

Third Row: (Cont.)

4th-6th, Men	2.50-4.00 ea.
7th and 8th, Men (red and brown)	6.00-8.00 ea.
9th and 10th, Men	7.50-10.00 ea.
11th, Man holding flower (red)	10.00-12.50

Fourth Row:

1st, Man w/violin, 8⅛" (**L D** in flower face emblem)	35.00-45.00
2nd, Man w/tricorn hat, 9⅝" (red)	40.00-50.00
3rd and 4th, Mandolin players, 10⅛" (red)	50.00-65.00 ea.
5th, Man w/blue coat and tricorn hat, 10⅝"	65.00-85.00
6th, Swashbuckler, 10" (red)	50.00-60.00

FIGURINES – SINGLE WOMEN

I have often wondered why so many of the ladies depicted by the Japanese seem to be fighting a strong head wind. Note the second ladies in the top row and bottom row. I have always called this style "wind swept" for lack of a better description.

The rest of the women shown here seem to be dancers except the third lady in the fourth row who may be swooning. Some of the dancers may have had partners, but not when I found them.

Ballerinas are a popular collectible. Those with skirts made of crinoline are the most desirable, but these are often damaged. A little damage seems not to matter to collectors, but lots of damage is a no-no!

Top Row:
    1st, Lady holding dress, 4¼" (red) $10.00-12.50
    2nd, Lady holding hat, 5" (red)   12.50-15.00
    3rd, Lady holding skirt (red)   15.00-17.50
    4th, Lady in curtsy (red)   12.50-15.00

Second Row:
    1st, Ballerina, 3⅝" ("Ucagco China" w/emblem; gold)   17.50-20.00
    2nd, Ballerina, green dress (red)   20.00-25.00
    3rd, Ballerina, 4¼" ("Sapu Fancy China")   20.00-25.00
    4th, Ballerina, 3½"   20.00-22.50

Third Row:
    1st, Dancer, blue dress, 4"   6.00- 8.00
    2nd, Dancer, yellow dress, 3½"   5.00- 6.00
    3rd and 5th, Dancers, 2½"   2.50- 4.00 ea.
    4th, Dancer, 3"   4.00- 5.00
    6th, Dancer w/leg exposed, 4"   6.00- 8.00

Fourth Row:
    1st, Dancer, orange dress, 3¼"   5.00- 6.00
    2nd, Dancer, 2½" (red)   2.50- 4.00
    3rd, Dancer (green)   2.00- 3.00
    4th-7th, Dancers   2.50- 4.00 ea.

Fifth Row:
    1st, Ballerina, 5¾" (red)   25.00-35.00
    2nd, Wind swept lady, 6½"   20.00-25.00
    3rd, Lady holding dress, 6¼" (red)   20.00-25.00
    4th, Ballerina w/turquoise skirt, 6¼" (red)   30.00-40.00

GLASS, ICON, INCENSE BURNERS and INKWELLS

Glass objects are difficult to find marked "Occupied Japan" because many of these objects were marked with paper labels. Perfume and cologne bottles as well as atomizers were usually embossed in the glass; so these can be found more readily. A major problem when finding these items are the daubers and bulbs which have been broken or are missing.

All small glass animals I have seen marked have had paper labels. Unfortunately if no label is found, it is impossible to prove its origin.

Incense burners come in a multitude of shapes. This is the first time I have found elephant burners to picture. In fact, the two Mexican burners are the first I have seen of non Oriental figurines. I have not been able to find out if the black incense burner in the third row was intended to be a black or not. I have never talked to anyone who has heard of this particular piece.

The dragon burner is not marked MIOJ, but came from a set of this pattern where the other pieces were marked.

The inkwell in the bottom row is a beauty!

Top Row:
1st and 2nd, Elephant sets (paper label)	$25.00-35.00 ea.
3rd and 5th, Blue atomizers (embossed)	25.00-30.00 ea.
4th, Blue perfume (embossed)	20.00-25.00
5th, Icon, 5⅛" (blue)	30.00-40.00

Second Row:
1st, 2nd and 5th, Perfumes w/dauber, 3½" (embossed)	20.00-25.00 ea.
3rd, Crystal perfume w/dauber (embossed)	17.50-20.00
4th, Salt shaker, 2⅜" (paper label)	10.00-12.50
6th, Blue goose (paper label on wing)	6.00- 8.00

Third Row:
1st, Incense burner, 4¼" (red)	17.50-20.00
2nd, Same except 4"	17.50-20.00
3rd, Same as 1st except (crown emblem)	17.50-20.00
4th, Black incense burner (red)	30.00-40.00
5th, White elephant incense burner (red)	17.50-20.00

Fourth Row:
1st, Incense burner, 4¼"	17.50-20.00
2nd, Dragon incense burner (no mark)	12.50-15.00
3rd and 4th, Mexican Incense burners (red)	25.00-30.00 ea.
5th, Elephant incense burner ("Ucagco China emblem")	25.00-35.00

Fifth Row:
1st, Modern ink well (paper label, "Osborne, Clifton N.J. Trademark)	12.50-15.00
2nd, China inkwell ("Andrea, H.P.")	60.00-75.00

JEWELRY

This is the first Occupied Japan book that I have found enough jewelry to make a separate category for it. The awareness of collectible jewelry has made some impact upon our market.

The strands of pearls were packaged ten to a pack with a paper label on each strand. Over the years most of these labels have probably been destroyed on similar beads you might find.

The "Butterfly Brooch" card is similar to one that I have shown before, but that one said "Brooch" only on the card. The "Butterfly Brooch" cards have two dozen butterflies, but the "Brooch" cards only had a dozen. The butterflies clip on to your clothing by folding up the wings to open the pin.

Notice the large amount of celluloid jewelry. In three books I have never shown a piece, but I found celluloid jewelry in three different states this time.

The green shamrock in the bottom row was to protect you from getting pinched on St. Patrick's Day.

Top Row:

1st, Strand of pearls (paper label)	$ 10.00-12.50 ea.
Package of 10	50.00-60.00
2nd, "Butterfly Brooch," card of 24	30.00-40.00
3rd, Strand of pearls (paper label)	12.50-15.00
4th, Strand of miniature beads (paper label)	15.00-17.50

Second Row:

1st, Rhinestone bracelet, "Lady Patricia" incised	30.00-50.00
2nd, Rhinestone bracelet, "Astra" incised	30.00-50.00
3rd, Crossed swords pin (embossed **T** in shield)	12.50-15.00
4th-8th, Celluloid pins (purple)	8.00-10.00 ea.

Third Row:

1st, Scottie dog in sweater, celluloid pin (incised)	12.50-15.00
2nd, Dog head, celluloid pin (incised)	10.00-12.50
3rd-5th, Celluloid bird pins (incised)	10.00-12.50 ea.

Fourth Row:

1st and 6th, Two dog head pins (incised)	10.00-12.50 ea.
2nd-4th, Celluloid brooch and earring set (incised)	20.00-25.00
5th, Shamrock (paper label)	2.50- 4.00

LACQUERWARE

Some of the most decorative items found in Occupied Japan are the lacquerware items. The ornate designs on the box lids and the vases are reminiscent of the fine art of cloisonne.

There is a gold and "pearl finish" stork on the ice bucket. The 13" vase is adorned with a fern type leaf design. Most of the pieces shown are marked "Maruni."

Top Row:

1st, Ice bucket, 7⅝" ("Maruni, Patented Lacquerware"; gold)	$ 40.00- 50.00
2nd, Vase w/leaf design, 13" ("Maruni, Patented Lacquerware"; gold)	100.00-115.00
3rd, Plate w/pagoda scene ("Maruni" 57-12)	30.00- 40.00

Second Row:

1st, Black box, 5½" x 9" ("Maruni")	50.00- 65.00
2nd, Five leaf clover tray ("Maruni")	40.00- 50.00
3rd, Red box ("Maruni")	50.00- 65.00

Third Row:

1st, Candy tray w/metal handle ("Maruni")	20.00- 25.00
2nd, Cup w/rattan handle ("Maruni")	15.00- 17.50
3rd, Piano (Occupied **R B** Japan)	40.00- 50.00
4th and 5th, Vases ("Maruni")	30.00- 40.00 ea.
6th, Basket ("Maruni")	50.00- 65.00

LAMPS

Occupied Japan lamps seem to occur only in pairs. Finding a missing mate to your lamp is a difficult task at best. Pairs are usually opposites. If a man is on one lamp, then the mate is usually a woman. If a couple make up one lamp, the other lamp has the couple in opposite places.

The pair of lamps in the top row are different than any I have shown before. There are two separate figurines applied to the metal base on each lamp instead of a single figurine of a couple. You have to check four figurines for damage instead of two.

On lamps with metal bases, the figurines have to be removed to see the Occupied Japan marks on the porcelain bottoms. Most of the figurines are drilled and fastened onto the base with a bolt, but if they are glued on the metal base - you have a problem! The cords for the lamps are hidden so you can better view each lamp.

By the same token, shades have also been removed so the figurines are not obscured from view. I get a few letters each year wanting to know what the original shades look like. They are usually a cheaply made plastic like material which are normally beat up from years of use. A few of the more ornate lamps have been found with silk shades.

Lamp measurements are to socket.

Top Row:
1st and 3rd, Colonial pair (porcelain bases marked in red)	$70.00-85.00
2nd, Lamp, 8⅜" w/pair applied roses one side/single on other (blue)	35.00-40.00

Second Row:
1st and 2nd, Colonial couple, 7⅛" (blue)	55.00-70.00 pr.
3rd, Colonial couple, 7⅝" t. x 5⅛" w. (red)	27.50-35.00
4th, Lamp same as 3rd except 7½" t. x 5" w. (red)	25.00-32.50

Third Row:
1st, Colonial couple seated	25.00-35.00
2nd, Man with urn	30.00-40.00
3rd, Colonial pair ("Chikusa" green **D** emblem with arrow-like bottom of **D**)	27.50-35.00

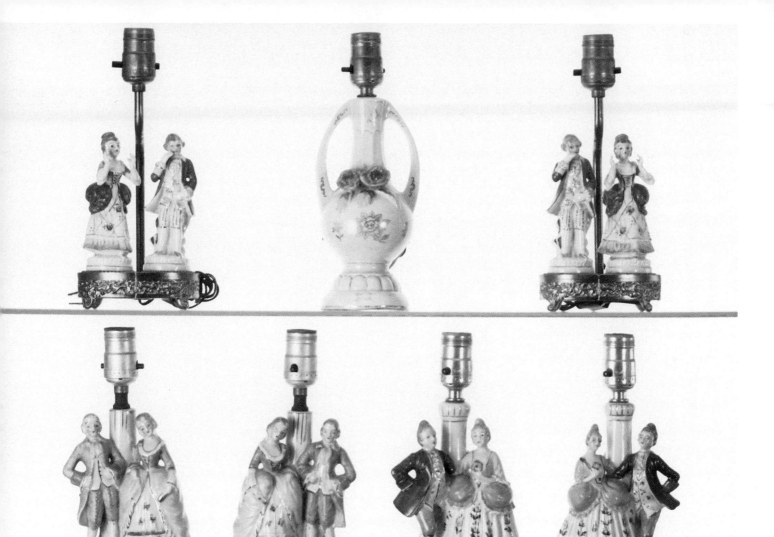

LORELEI, MERMAIDS and OTHER FISH BOWL DECORATIONS

In Greek mythology Lorelei was the siren who lured sailors to death on the rocks. I am not sure these little nude sirens are capable of that, but they are cute. These little sirens (3" to 3½") are not found often today. All the ones pictured were collected years ago.

Mermaids also have mythological charms. As a boy, I can still remember going to Webb's City (a Florida tourist trap) to see my first "real" mermaid. Even then, I was disappointed that she did not look "real" to me. Collectors have always sought out these half fish and half woman items. Many of these are very fragile and have been broken over the years. Even my mother-in-law destroyed a couple while we were trying to sort out items for the photography session.

Do you know how long it takes to go through 10,000 pieces of Occupied Japan? We had to unpack each piece and sort them into categories to photograph for the book. It took over a week and the house became an Occupied Japan museum during the process. Each piece had to be checked to make sure it was not pictured in the previous three books. A few pieces were redone if they were part of a set or pair that had not previously been shown complete.

Top Row:
    1st, Lorelei bud vase ("Mocco"; pineapple w/wings
        emblem; red) $ 8.00-10.00
    2nd, Lorelei planter (red)   10.00-12.50
    3rd, Lorelei w/cello (red)   8.00-10.00
    4th, Lorelei bud vase ("Mocco"; red)   8.00-10.00
    5th-7th, Lorelei w/violin, drum or accordion (red)   8.00-10.00 ea.

Second Row:
    1st, Orange tail mermaid on rocks (red)   20.00-22.50
    2nd, Blue tail mermaid on rocks (red)   20.00-22.50
    3rd, Same as 2nd only unpainted (red)   17.50-20.00
    4th, Bisque, 3½", orange tail   20.00-22.50
    5th and 6th, Lorelei bud vases ("Mocco"; red)   8.00-10.00 ea.

Third Row:
    1st and 2nd, Same as 4th in second row (green/blue tail)   20.00-22.50 ea.
    3rd, Mermaid holding blue tail (red)   20.00-22.50
    4th, Mermaid sitting w/orange tail (red)   20.00-25.00
    5th, Bisque mermaid w/small blue tipped tail (red)   20.00-22.50
    6th and 7th, Reclining bisque mermaids, 4⅜"   25.00-30.00 ea.

Fourth Row:
    1st and 3rd, Fish bowl pagodas (red)   10.00-12.50 ea.
    2nd and 4th, Mermaid sitters (red)   17.50-20.00 ea.
    5th, Mermaid on shell (red)   20.00-25.00
    6th, Pagoda   6.00- 8.00

Fifth Row:
    1st, 4th and 5th, Fish bowl pagodas (red)   10.00-12.50 ea.
    2nd and 3rd, Fish bowl pagodas   10.00-12.50 ea.

METAL – MOSTLY ASH TRAYS

Metallic objects marked Occupied Japan are generally among the least collected items of our genre. While there are few pieces I can honestly say are a "beauty to behold," there are many very "interesting" objects to be found. There are a **few** collectors of "metal only" Occupied Japan.

In the next three photographs I will endeavor to pique your interest.

Top Row:

1st, Buddha tray (embossed)	$ 8.00-10.00
2nd, New York City souvenir tray (embossed)	5.00- 6.00
3rd, Ornate serving tray (embossed)	12.50-15.00

Second Row:

1st, Louisiana souvenir tray (embossed)	4.00- 5.00
2nd, New York heart w/Statue of Liberty (embossed)	10.00-12.50
3rd, 5th and 6th, Ash trays (embossed backwards)	2.00-3.00 ea.
4th, Ash tray (embossed)	2.50- 4.00

Third Row:

1st, Candy – three part (embossed **T** in a chicken shaped emblem)	10.00-12.50
2nd, Florida souvenir tray (embossed)	4.00- 5.00
3rd, Chicago souvenir tray ("Pico - 1074" embossed)	4.00- 5.00
4th, Ornate gold colored ash tray (embossed **PG** in parallelogram)	4.00- 5.00
5th, Ornate silver plated ash tray (embossed)	5.00- 6.00

Fourth Row:

1st, Oval tray (embossed)	5.00- 6.00
2nd, Ash tray w/peacock (embossed)	2.50- 4.00
3rd, Six piece cigarette set (embossed)	20.00-25.00
4th, Yellowstone Park souvenir tray (embossed **SNK** in parallelogram)	4.00- 5.00

Fifth Row:

1st, Colorado souvenir tray ("Pico - 2748" embossed)	4.00- 5.00
2nd, Howe Cabins NY ("Enco 2T391" embossed)	4.00- 5.00
3rd, Ornate blue ash tray (embossed "Rich Barry silverplated")	4.00- 5.00
4th, Six piece miniature tea set (embossed)	20.00-25.00
5th, El Paso c. 1950 (embossed MIOJ in banner)	5.00- 6.00

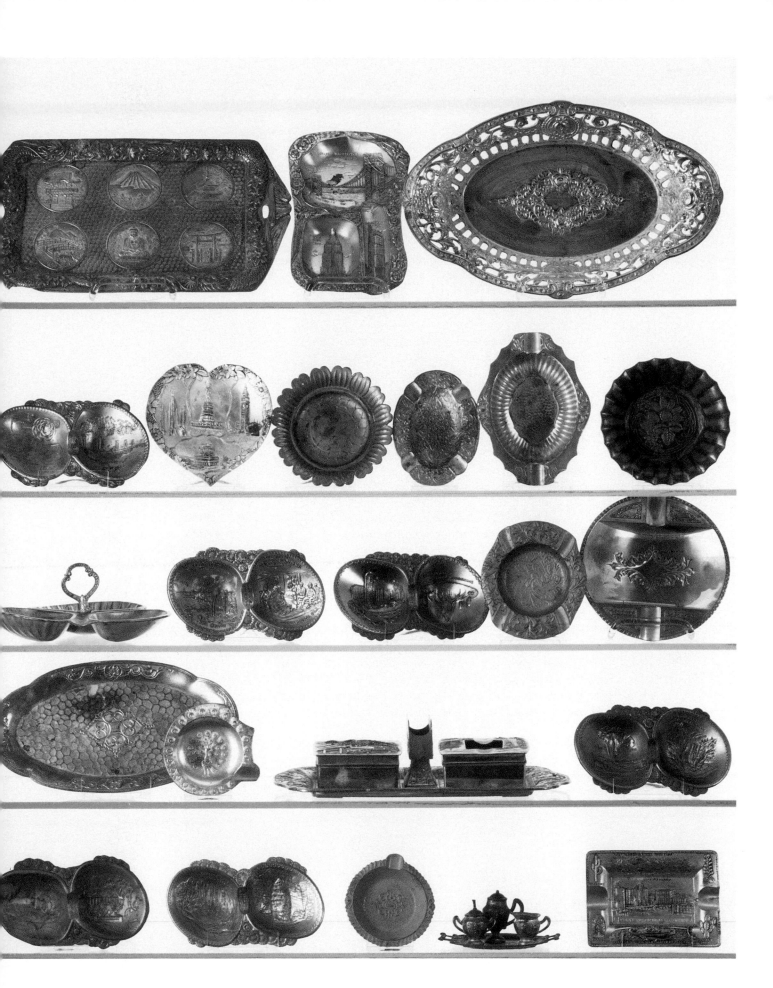

METAL – MOSTLY CIGARETTE LIGHTERS

I try to be very picky about metal selections for the book. Trying to show interesting and quality metallic objects MIOJ is a problem. It is fairly easy to pick up some of the more commonly found ash trays and souvenir items, but after that it becomes a challenge.

The collectors who do search for metallic Occupied Japan pieces are also very choosey and that makes for some heated competition!

A couple of the lighters shown here were entertaining trying to find the secret to "sparking their wicks." The rocket ship in the second row has to have its wings adjusted to strike the flint. The radio in the fourth row has to have one of its knobs moved to pop its top.

Most of these lighters still "spark" and with a little lighter fluid you can still light someone's fire.

Top Row:
    1st, Ash tray; real butterfly encased/glass bottom;
        lighter/side (embossed) $20.00-22.50
    2nd, Celluloid piano (embossed)   20.00-25.00
    3rd, Metal piano (embossed)   17.50-20.00
    4th, "Photolite Table Lighter Pat P7844127171639 Oriental
        Co. Ltd MTR Toys" (embossed)   25.00-35.00
    5th, Golf ball lighter (embossed)   12.50-15.00

Second Row:
    1st, Knight lighter (embossed on shield)   10.00-12.50
    2nd, Knight lighter (embossed on base)   10.00-12.50
    3rd, Camel lighter (embossed on base)   15.00-17.50
    4th, Elephant lighter (embossed on tummy)   15.00-17.50
    5th, Rocket ship lighter (embossed on base)   20.00-25.00
    6th, Scottie dog lighter (embossed on base w/ship emblem)   15.00-17.50

Third Row:
    1st, Fish lighter (embossed "Continental New York
        Silverplate MIOJ")   12.50-15.00
    2nd, Desk lighter (embossed bird symbol)   5.00- 6.00
    3rd, Normal style lighter (imprinted on bottom)   4.00- 5.00
    4th, Aladdin type lighter (embossed)   6.00- 8.00
    5th, Lighter (embossed basket w/**PKS** in parallelogram)   5.00- 6.00
    6th, Desk lighter (embossed **LK** in bell emblem)   6.00- 8.00

Fourth Row:
    1st, Peacock lighter (embossed)   10.00-12.50
    2nd, Fancy dragon six piece cigarette set (embossed tray) 25.00-35.00
    3rd, Floor model radio lighter (imprinted Pat P No 1543
        on base)   20.00-25.00
    4th, Barrel "Chicago" (embossed)   10.00-12.50

Fifth Row:
    1st, Horse head lighter "**K1** world w/wings emblem" **C.M.C.**
        N.Y. Silver Plate (embossed)   12.50-15.00
    2nd, Horse head lighter (embossed)   12.50-15.00
    3rd, Horse head lighter (embossed "**C.M.C.** Silver Plate MIOJ") 12.50-15.00
    4th, Boot lighter with ash tray (boot and tray embossed)   8.00-10.00
    5th, Two boots w/hat ash tray and tray to hold all
        (embossed heels, hat and tray w/cloverleaf emblem)   15.00-17.50 set

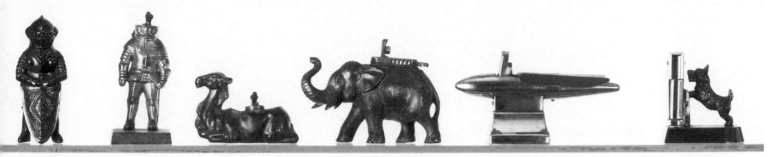

METALLIC OBJECTS

There are a multitude of metal jewelry and cigarette boxes that are MIOJ. Some of these are attractive enough to be displayed while others ought to be buried in the nearest landfill.

The most desirable metal piece of Occupied Japan is the bird cage clock in the second row. It even keeps fairly accurate time after all these years! It is not quite as bad as a cuckoo, but that bird does keep on ticking!

Top Row:

1st, Basket, "**HKK** in diamond emblem" impressed on foot $	17.50- 20.00
2nd, Floral vase (embossed "Miami Beach, Fla." on base)	12.50- 15.00
3rd, Urn vase (embossed)	10.00- 12.50
4th, Copper urn vase w/grapes (embossed)	12.50- 15.00
5th, Container w/lid (embossed) Probably had glass insert at one time	12.50- 15.00

Second Row:

1st, Bird cage clock (impressed)	125.00-200.00
2nd, Bowl w/three angel feet (embossed)	12.50- 15.00
3rd and 4th, Sugar/creamer set (embossed **M** in tree emblem)	20.00- 22.50

Third Row:

1st, Red ring box w/pink interior (embossed)	10.00- 12.50
2nd, Dragon cigarette box and tray (embossed)	12.50- 15.00
3rd, Box (embossed "Nippo" w/**Y** in diamond emblem)	10.00- 12.50

Fourth Row:

1st, Ink well w/pen holder; red and black well inserts (embossed)	15.00- 17.50
2nd, Bowl, 4 footed w/lid (embossed)	12.50- 15.00
3rd, Heart box (embossed)	10.00- 12.50
4th, Box w/peacock on red background (embossed w/flag; **CKS** in emblem)	15.00- 17.50

Fifth Row:

1st, Candy compote (embossed **KT** emblem)	10.00- 12.50
2nd, Cowboy hat and glove top (embossed **Y** emblem)	8.00- 10.00
3rd, Lockable box (embossed **ZU** in crown emblem)	12.50- 15.00
4th, Small box w/peacock on red background (embossed **HS** emblem)	8.00- 10.00

MISCELLANEOUS SERVING DISHES

The Japanese copied many of the popular types of English and European china. The corn dishes were a popular English Staffordshire design that even an American pottery company, Shawnee, also copied. After seeing the fruit basket in the third row, I wondered if these were copies of English or copies of the American Shawnee. If you happen to know any more about this, let me know.

The lobster dishes in the bottom row are examples of copying Royal Bayreuth China. The sugar bowl takes a lid that lines up the top of the lobster with its tail. The three part serving dish uses a lobster for the handle.

Top Row:

1st, Creamer (green)	$ 8.00-10.00
2nd, Corn sugar w/lid	12.50-15.00
3rd, Corn creamer	8.00-10.00
4th, Corn marmalade (green)	12.50-15.00
5th, Flower basket embossed cookie jar (embossed MIOJ "SAMPLE")	20.00-25.00

Second Row:

1st, Rice bowl, colorful (turquoise)	6.00- 8.00
2nd, Tea cup (blue)	6.00- 8.00
3rd, Corn marmalade	15.00-17.50
4th, Tea cup, bird scene (red)	7.50-10.00
5th, Rice bowl, floral (green)	5.00- 6.00
6th, Orange marmalade	12.50-15.00

Third Row:

1st, Pink Lily of Valley sugar	10.00-12.50
2nd, Soup spoon (red)	10.00-12.50
3rd, Corn container (blue)	4.00- 5.00
4th, Fruit basket (**T** in circle)	20.00-22.50
5th, Basket weave butter dish (**T** in circle)	17.50-20.00
6th, Egg cup	6.00- 8.00

Fourth Row:

1st, Saki cup in front	5.00- 6.00
2nd, Ship rice bowl (red)	6.00- 8.00
3rd, 5th, 7th and 9th, Saki cups (green)	5.00- 6.00 ea.
4th, Dragon rice bowl (red)	7.50-10.00
6th, Large rice bowl (red)	8.00-10.00
8th, Red floral rice bowl (red)	7.50-10.00
10th, Large rice bowl ("ISCO" in Diamond; red)	8.00-10.00

Fifth Row:

1st, Iris small creamer (green)	10.00-12.50
2nd, Small 4 footed floral oval bowl (orange)	5.00- 6.00
3rd, Saki cup	4.00- 5.00
4th, Lobster sugar w/lid	25.00-32.50
5th, Lobster creamer	15.00-17.50
6th, Lobster 3-part tray	25.00-35.00

MUGS, PAPER and SEWING ITEMS

There are two different sets of people-handled mugs. Cowboy-handled mugs have a horseshoe on the side opposite the handle while the "Howdy Doody" looking characters have a steer head opposite the handle. The metal mugs (nickel plated) in third row were supposedly made from a battleship's parts. Two picture hunters; one shows Presidio Ave., Ca. which I assume is San Fransisco and the other is a map of Philippines Papua.

On Page 88 are some children's books for transferring pictures. I had never seen these made in Occupied Japan before, but I remember working with this type of book as a child. On Page 89 in the second row are paper noise makers which still work when you squeeze them. **Most paper products are stamped Occupied Japan in purple or blue ink.**

Page 91

Top Row:

1st, Cowboy being "booted" by lady mug (red)	$20.00-25.00
2nd, Cowboy mug	20.00-22.50
3rd, Santa mug (red)	30.00-35.00
4th, Brown elephant mug, 4¾"	17.50-20.00

Second Row:

1st-4th, People mugs (**L.D.** in cloud red or orange marks)	20.00-22.50 ea.

Third Row:

1st-4th, Nickel plated 5" mugs made from ship's parts (see above)	35.00-50.00 ea.

Fourth Row:

1st, Indian head mug	10.00-12.50
2nd and 3rd, Small mugs (red)	5.00- 6.00 ea.
4th, Cupids w/bow ("Toru Brand"; blue)	10.00-12.50

Page 92

1st, Large umbrella open on left and folded in front (22" before open)	25.00-35.00 ea.
2nd, Open umbrella on right	12.50-15.00
3rd, "Transfer Picture" books intact	30.00-50.00 ea.
4th, Floral fans	12.00-20.00 ea.
5th, Large black fan (white)	20.00-25.00
6th, Small black fan (white)	12.50-15.00

Page 93

Top Row:

1st, Leaves (paper label)	2.50- 4.00
2nd and 4th, Party favors, 6"	5.00- 6.00 ea.
3rd, 4th etc., Party horns (paper label)	5.00- 6.00 ea.

Second Row:

1st, "Spot The Spot" puzzle (red)	6.00- 8.00
2nd-8th, Noise makers	2.50- 4.00 ea.
9th and 10th, Drink paper umbrellas (paper label)	1.00- 1.50 ea.

Third Row:

1st, "Old Glory" bow tie (paper label)	5.00- 6.00
2nd, Pin box (embossed)	7.50-10.00
3rd, Celluloid basket tape measure	20.00-25.00
4th and 5th, Needle packs	8.00-10.00 ea.
6th and 7th, Celluloid pig tape measure	20.00-22.50 ea.
8th and 9th, Colonial couple pin cushions (red)	8.00-10.00 ea.

Fourth Row:

1st and 2nd, Cat or dog pin cushion (arch emblem)	5.00- 6.00 ea.
3rd and 4th, Half-doll pin cushions	30.00-35.00 ea.
5th-8th, Colonial pin cushions (red)	8.00-10.00 ea.

Fifth Row:

1st-5th, Cat and dog pin cushions (arch emblem)	6.00- 8.00 ea.
6th, Oriental lady pin cushion, 6" (red)	12.50-15.00

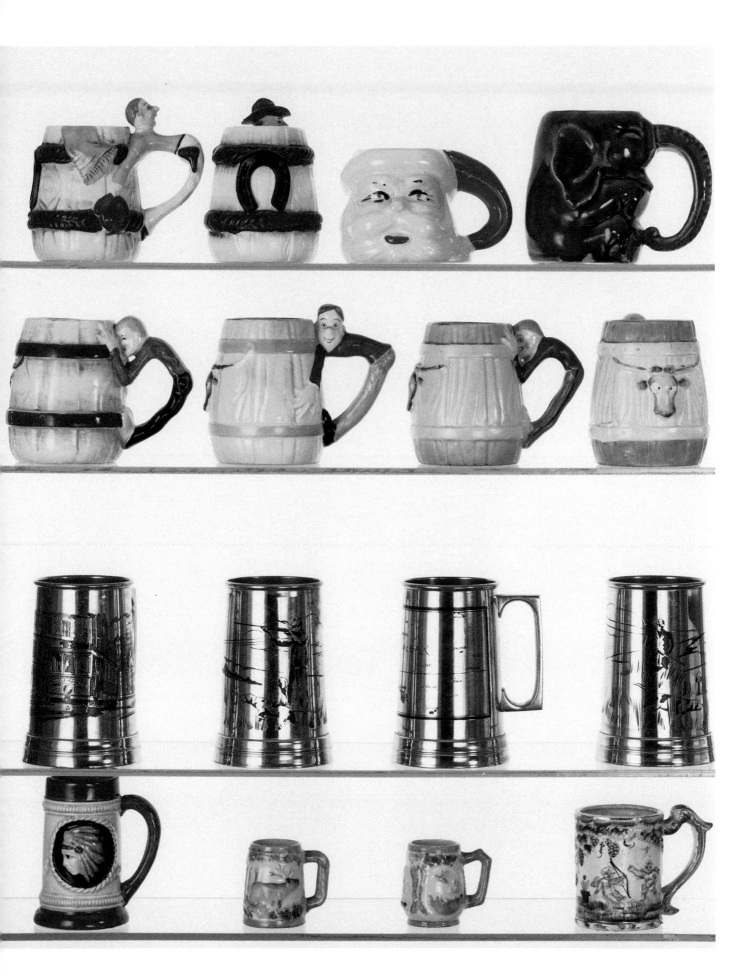

PLANTERS – ANIMAL

There are many animals represented by planters, but the most popular was the donkey. Where the Japanese got the idea for **green** donkeys is beyond me. Note the bird circle planters in the top row of Page 95 and the parrot in the top row of Page 97. These attach to a 24" porcelain chain for hanging.

Page 95

Top Row:

1st, Parrot (**T** over top of **M**)	$15.00-17.50
2nd and 3rd, Hanging bird planters w/24" chain (arch emblem)	35.00-50.00 ea.
4th, Bird planter	7.50-10.00

Second Row:

1st-4th, Elephant planters; white, pink, green and blue (arch emblem)	12.50-15.00 ea.

Third Row:

1st, White elephant planter	5.00- 6.00
2nd and 4th, Rearing elephants (arch emblem)	8.00-10.00 ea.
3rd, Brown elephant (blue)	12.50-15.00
5th and 6th, Smaller versions of second row (arch emblem)	7.50-10.00 ea.

Fourth Row:

1st and 2nd, Birds on fence (green) and cow	6.00- 8.00 ea.
3rd and 4th, Pig or frog	12.50-15.00 ea.

Fifth Row:

1st-3rd, Elephant or bird planters	8.00-10.00 ea.
4th, Bear on blue tree (arch emblem)	10.00-12.50
5th, Blue squirrel (brown)	8.00-10.00

Page 96

Dark green mark second row, 2nd
Brown marks: second row, 3rd; third row, 1st; fourth row, 2nd; fifth row; 1st.

Large donkey	10.00-12.50 ea.
Medium donkeys	6.00- 8.00 ea.
Smaller donkeys	3.00- 5.00 ea.

Page 97

Top Row:

1st and 2nd, Lambs (arch emblem)	6.00- 8.00 ea.
3rd, Hanging Parrot	30.00-35.00
4th, Parrot	12.50-15.00
5th, Hanging parrot w/24" chain ("Maruhonware" **K** in circle)	50.00-65.00

Second Row:

1st-3rd, Lambs (arch emblem) (medium - Pat App 1251); (large Pat App 1259)	12.50-15.00 set
4th, Lamb	2.50- 4.00
5th, Pink bunny (embossed SSK 105)	10.00-12.50
6th and 7th, Bunnies (arch emblem)	10.00-12.50 ea.

Third Row:

1st, Woodpecker eyeing frog	4.00- 5.00
2nd-4th, Birds (green or orange)	6.00- 8.00 ea.
5th, Green donkey	6.00- 8.00

Fourth Row:

1st, Medium donkey	6.00- 8.00
2nd-8th, except 6th (red or black)	3.00- 5.00 ea.
6th, Donkey ("Morkinware" fancy **M**; brown)	4.00- 5.00

Fifth Row:

1st, Zebra (arch emblem)	6.00- 8.00
2nd, Dog cart (red)	5.00- 6.00
3rd, Very small donkey cart	2.00- 3.00
4th and 5th, Cow carts (brown)	7.50-10.00 ea.
6th, Cow planter	6.00-8.00

PLANTERS – PEOPLE

I probably should have subtitled this "ethnic" planters as there are quite a few cultures represented here. After purchasing new Occupied Japan for three years for this book, it is amazing to me how many different planters have been accumulated. Prices for planters remain reasonable; so you could put a large collection together without having to mortgage the homestead.

The different ways that figurines were incorporated into the planters is astounding. Many times you have to look from behind or above to determine that it truly is a planter. It is a well designed planter that makes you look for the opening!

Top Row:
1st and 2nd, Oriental girl and boy by bamboo tree, 4⅛"	$ 7.50-10.00 ea.
3rd, Head planter (H.P.)	10.00-12.50
4th and 5th, Oriental boy and girl, 5" (red)	12.50-15.00 ea.
6th, Big hat Oriental, 5⅛" (red)	6.00- 8.00
7th, Shelf sitter planter	12.50-15.00

Second Row:
1st, Seated mandolin player (**K** in circle)	6.00- 8.00
2nd and 3rd, Boy w/rickshaw	10.00-12.50 ea.
4th, Oriental couple ("Rossetti, Chicago, U.S.A., H.P.; blue)	15.00-17.50
5th, Carriage boy	4.00- 5.00

Third Row:
1st, Heart w/angel, 3⅝" (red)	8.00-10.00
2nd, Umbrella girl (H.P.)	6.00- 8.00
3rd, Chicken feeding boy (H.P.)	6.00- 8.00
4th, Girl reading book (blue)	8.00-10.00
5th, Girl w/accordion (red)	4.00- 5.00
6th, Colonial man, 4⅝", "Catalina" on side	10.00-12.50

Fourth Row:
1st and 2nd, Dutch boy and girl, 4½"	12.50-15.00 ea.
3rd, Girl matches 6th in row above, "Catalina" on side	10.00-12.50
4th, Couple	4.00- 5.00
5th, girl w/urn (red)	5.00- 6.00
6th, Boy playing ukelele (blue)	8.00-10.00

Fifth Row:
1st and 2nd, Boy and girl on fence w/dog, 4¾"	8.00-10.00 ea.
3rd, Dutch girl w/buckets (red)	8.00-10.00
4th, Girl w/duck after nose, 4⅝" (red)	6.00- 8.00
5th, Sleepy Mexican (red)	8.00-10.00

PLAQUES and WOOD

There are a wide variety of wall plaques available in Occupied Japan. Shown here is the widest assortment that I have ever been able to accumulate for a book. The most collectible is the "Hummel Type" angel in the top row. The flamingo in the top row differs from the hanging planters shown earlier. The back of this plaque is flat to hang against the wall where the earlier versions shown are rounded on both sides.

We had difficulty in balancing the parrot in the second row and had to place her (had to be a "her" to create as much a problem as she did) sideways in order to get it on a shelf.

The wooden bird on box in third row is a butt retriever for those wanting to smoke themselves to death. In the fourth row is a dog house with rubber dog attached to a bulb that, when squeezed, sends the dog out to visit.

Top Row:

1st, Oriental vase, flattened to fit wall (green)	$ 12.50-15.00
2nd, Oriental girl ("Mot Jama"; brown)	15.00-17.50
3rd, "Hummel Type" angel	50.00-60.00
4th, Peacock wall pocket	20.00-22.50
5th, Flamingo wall plaque (red)	20.00-25.00

Second Row:

1st, Wooden ship	12.50-15.00
2nd and 3rd, Small flattened cornucopias (red)	4.00- 5.00 ea.
4th, Iris wall pocket	12.50-15.00
5th, Rose on black wall plaque ("Hadson" anchor symbol)	12.50-15.00
6th, Parrot wall pocket	30.00-35.00
7th, Cup and saucer holder	2.50- 4.00

Third Row:

1st, Wooden cigarette box, bird retriever (**N** in circle)	30.00-40.00
2nd, Wooden cigarette box (blue)	20.00-25.00
3rd, Wooden rickshaw	12.50-15.00
4th, Bamboo handled tray (red)	20.00-22.50

Fourth Row:

1st, Wooden spoon	8.00-10.00
2nd, "Dime into penny" magic trick box	20.00-22.50
3rd, Dog house with rubber jumping dog (rubber bulb marked)	8.00-10.00
4th, Decorative straw basket (blue)	35.00-45.00

Fifth Row:

1st, Apple wall plaque	8.00-10.00
2nd and 4th, Mallard plaques	15.00-17.50 ea.
3rd, Pipe cleaner man	12.50-15.00
5th, Green horse plaque	17.50-20.00
6th, Dutch boy (plaster)?	20.00-22.50

SALT and PEPPER SHAKERS (METAL)

I did not have a large accumulation of ceramic salt and pepper shakers for this book. Unfortunately, those items had already been sold out of the huge collection I bought. However, I do have a variety of metallic. The collector who bought the shakers obviously was not interested in the metallic shakers.

At some point, someone taped down the lid of the red boxed set in the first row and peeled off some of the box. The set is intact; so that is no great problem. It just makes one wonder at the mentality of someone who would tape the top of a paper box which has a perfectly good working metal clasp.

Top Row:

1st, Cobalt blue shakers and mustard w/spoon on tray in box (embossed)	$40.00-45.00
2nd, Urns w/tray (embossed)	20.00-22.50
3rd, Set w/cobalt blue shakers, sugar, tray, chop stick and spoon (embossed Pat #93399)	40.00-45.00

Second Row:

1st, Coffee pot set (embossed K1)	12.50-15.00
2nd, Skillet, flowers on tray (embossed)	20.00-22.50
3rd, Urns on tray (embossed)	15.00-17.50
4th, Teapots on tray (embossed "Delco silver plated")	15.00-17.50
5th, Penguins (embossed)	20.00-22.50

Third Row:

1st, Tall gold colored shakers (embossed)	15.00-17.50
2nd, Box and shakers to its right (embossed)	20.00-22.50 set

Fourth Row:

1st, Cocktail shakers on tray (impressed)	20.00-22.50
2nd, Single elephant (embossed)	12.50-15.00
3rd, Single urn (embossed)	5.00- 6.00
4th, Souvenir "Washington, D.C." shakers	12.50-15.00
5th, Candles on tray (impressed)	20.00-22.50
6th, Single coffee pot (embossed)	6.00- 8.00

Fifth Row:

1st, Cowboy boots (embossed mark inside heel)	12.50-15.00
2nd, Egg set; cup and shakers (Souvenir of Yellowstone Park)	20.00-25.00
3rd, Lamp set (impressed)	12.50-15.00
4th, Ship (embossed)	20.00-22.50
5th, Single donkey piled w/prospector tools (embossed)	10.00-12.50

SETS

Every time you think you have found a complete set of the "Cottage" what should appear but additional pieces. I had never seen butter pats or the covered jar similar in size to the butter until I bought this set. All of this is patterned (copied) after the English set that was so very popular. I call the wicker handled jar a cookie jar, but to be proper it probably is a biscuit jar.

"Strawberry" sets remain popular with collectors. There are at least three different size sets and numerous Japanese companies who made these sets. The covered jar in the top row is probably a sugar. It is the only piece shown that has a marked company name, and that is "Rossetti" Chicago, U.S.A. That hardly qualifies for who actually made it!

The windmill set on the second row has previously been shown in a darker blue, but this set also has a smaller creamer. The creamers to these sets look as if they need a lid to complete the windmill, but I have never run across one with a lid. If you have one or see one with a cover, let me know. The shakers on the right side of the second row were found with the windmill teapot in the top row.

Top Row:
1st, Strawberry salt and pepper on leaf tray set	$ 20.00-25.00
2nd and 4th, Strawberry shakers, 3⅝"; holes form **S** or **P**	17.50-20.00
3rd, Strawberry covered sugar ("Rossetti", Chicago U.S.A.)	15.00-17.50
4th, Windmill teapot	35.00-45.00

Second Row:
1st, Windmill small creamer, 2⅝"	8.00-10.00
2nd, Windmill Sugar w/lid, 3⅞"	17.50-20.00
3rd, Windmill teapot, 4⅞"	35.00-40.00
4th, Windmill Large creamer, 2⅞"	8.00-10.00
5th, Salt and pepper set, found w/teapot in top row	12.50-15.00

Third Row: **Cottage pieces**
1st, Set: salt, pepper and mustard on tray (**T** in circle on tray)	30.00-35.00
2nd, Covered dish (**T** in circle)	25.00-30.00
3rd, Butter dish (**T** in circle)	35.00-40.00
4th-7th, Butter pats (**T** in circle)	10.00-12.50 ea.

Fourth Row: **Cottage pieces**
1st, Teapot (**T** in circle)	50.00-65.00
2nd, Cookie or biscuit jar (**T** in circle)	75.00-90.00
3rd, Sugar and creamer on tray (**T** in circle on each piece)	30.00-35.00

SHELF SITTERS

When shelf sitters come with benches, they are much easier to arrange. Have you noticed how many shelf sitter have a round hole in their bottoms. These were made to fit round pegs on benches. No problem getting these to si still for a photo. The first and second boys in the third row even have a wire to help hold them on a peg.

No matter how hard you try, there is no way you can get all of these to sit on the edge of the shelf. No wonder s many have been broken over the years trying to do that. I might suggest that if you put any of these out for sale, d not place them on the shelf edge of your display. We ran into that problem in an "Antique Mall" in Florida recently Those shelf sitters will "jump off" when you are trying to look at something else.

The tall boy reading a book in the top row and the ballerina in the fourth row are each 6⅛" tall. That is as large a most Occupied Japan shelf sitters are found. Occasionally, one will be found up to 6½". The ballerina is marke "Ucagco China" and is one of the best made shelf sitters I have ever owned.

Finding pairs of shelf sitters is a real challenge!

Top Row:

1st, Bisque fisherman, 5"	$17.50-20.00
2nd, Bisque fisherman (impressed on back)	12.50-15.00
3rd, Bisque fisherman (red)	12.50-15.00
4th, Book reader (red)	20.00-25.00
5th and 6th, Oriental pr. (red)	12.50 ea. or 27.50-30.00 pr.

Second Row:

1st, Girl w/red hat (broken), 5" if perfect	17.50-20.00
2nd, Boy holding hat	12.50-15.00
3rd and 4th, Colonial couple	8.50 ea. or 17.50-20.00 pr.
5th, Dutch girl	12.50-15.00
6th, Dutch boy (**M** in circle emblem)	12.50-15.00
7th, Girl w/ song book	10.00-12.50

Third Row:

1st, Boy w/horn, 3¾" (red)	10.00-12.50
2nd, Oriental boy (red)	12.50-15.00
3rd, Girl w/ruffles (blue)	15.00-17.50
4th, Girl w/doll, 5" (blue)	17.50-20.00
5th, Bisque couple (impressed on back)	10.00-12.50
6th, Girl w/flowers	10.00-12.50
7th, Boy playing banjo (blue)	8.00-10.00

Fourth Row:

1st, Ballerina, 6⅛" ("Ucagco China" w/emblem; red)	30.00-35.00
2nd, Boy (red)	10.00-12.50
3rd, Oriental playing mandolin (red)	10.00-12.50
4th, Oriental playing mandolin (red)	8.00-10.00
5th, Oriental	8.00-10.00
6th, Blue boy (blue)	8.00-10.00

Fifth Row:

1st, Girl in green dress, 3⅝"	8.00-10.00
2nd, Girl w/instrument (red)	10.00-12.50
3rd, Girl w/music book (green)	12.50-15.00
4th, Oriental w/musical instrument	10.00-12.50
5th, Bisque cowgirl ("Mose"; red)	12.50-15.00

SMALLS (PITCHERS, TEAPOTS and WATERING CANS)

These are some of the miniature pieces that are quickly gathered by doll collectors for doll houses and by collector of smalls who put them in "print type" boxes on the walls. Smaller items used to be hard to sell, but in the last fe years the "miniaturized" items have been "HOT!"

One good thing about the small items is that they do not take up a lot of display space as do many Occupied Japa collectibles. Even apartment dwellers can have a "smalls" collection.

Top Row:

1st, Pitcher w/yellow flower, 3⅛" (red)	$ 2.50- 4.00
2nd and 4th, Pitchers w/brown design	2.00- 3.00 ea.
3rd, Floral pitcher ("Rossetti" Chicago, U.S.A.; red)	4.00- 5.00
5th, Pitcher, 5⅛"	5.00- 6.00
6th, Green pitcher w/orange flower (red)	4.00- 5.00
7th, Blue pitcher w/draped lady (H.P. red rectangle in circle)	6.00- 8.00
8th, Pitcher w/basket weave design	2.50- 4.00

Second Row:

1st, Ornate water can, 3" ("Hokulosha" **H** in wreath emblem)	8.00-10.00
2nd, White can w/raised pink rose ("Maruyama"; red)	5.00- 6.00
3rd and 4th, White w/red rose (red) or basket weave (H.P.)	4.00- 5.00 ea.
5th, Floral can (red)	2.00- 3.00
6th, Yellow can w/raised rose	5.00- 6.00
7th, Blue can w/raised pink rose (red)	5.00- 6.00

Third Row:

1st and 12th, Coffee pots, 2" (red) (lid missing in photo) w/lid	4.00- 5.00 ea.
2nd-6th, 10th, Pitchers (red or black)	2.50- 4.00 ea.
7th-9th, Water cans (red)	2.00- 3.00 ea.
11th, Pitcher ("Pico"; red)	2.50- 4.00

Fourth Row:

1st, Pitcher, 2⅜", "Souvenir 1000 Islands, N.Y." (red)	2.50- 4.00
2nd, Ornate handle pitcher ("Rossetti" Chicago, U.S.A.; red)	5.00- 6.00
3rd, Small pitcher, 1¾" ("Pico"; red)	2.50- 4.00
4th, White pitcher w/white raised rose	2.50- 4.00
5th and 6th, Matching urns, 3⅛" (red)	2.50- 4.00 ea.
7th, White pitcher w/pink rose (red)	2.00- 3.00
8th and 9th, Blue and orange pitchers w/raised roses	5.00- 6.00 ea.
10th, Bird pitcher	10.00-12.50

Fifth Row:

1st, Water can, 1¾"	1.00- 1.50
2nd and 3rd, White floral or blue pitcher	2.50- 4.00 ea.
4th, Pitcher ("Pico"; red)	2.50- 4.00
5th, White teapot w/lid	5.00- 6.00
6th, Blue coffee w/raised pink flower and lid	7.50-10.00
7th, Same only teapot	6.00- 8.00
8th, Round teakettle w/lid	5.00- 6.00
9th, Coffee pot w/lid ("K. Ishihara"; red)	6.00- 8.00

TEA or COFFEE POTS and SETS

At present there appears to be a never ending supply of Occupied Japan teapots. Finding matching pieces t
complete the tea sets is another matter. Some tea sets come with a matching sugar and creamer while others do no
Perhaps those that do not have a sugar and creamer can be deemed chocolate sets; but I have never figured out ho
to tell the sets which **should** have a creamer and sugar and which do not. Most of the demitasse sets have creame
and sugars.

You can expect to pay a premium (more than the sum of the pieces) if you find a complete set!

While the brown glazed pottery types (shown in the bottom row) can be found with ease, I have never seen matchin
cup and saucer sets to go with them. That saves a lot of time looking for cups that the collectors who buy other set
have to spend.

Individual (or single cup) teapots are mostly found with the brown glaze finish, but there exceptions to that rule.

Top Row:
  Demitasse set consisting of six cup and saucers and
    coffee pot; floral w/gold rim ("Nasco" w/MIOJ in green
    wreath) $110.00-135.00
  Cup and saucer   10.00- 12.50 ea
  Teapot   40.00- 50.00

Second Row:
  1st, Gray teapot w/yellow blooming water lilies (red)   20.00- 25.00
  2nd, Demitasse cup and saucer with leaf design (blue)   8.00- 10.00
  3rd, Rust w/floral teapot (red)   20.00- 25.00

Third Row:
  Demitasse set consisting of six cup/saucers, creamer, sugar
    and coffee pot; fall tree scene (red)   145.00-175.00
  Cup and saucer   10.00- 12.50 ea.
  Creamer   10.00- 12.50
  Sugar w/lid   15.00- 17.50
  Teapot   50.00- 60.00

Fourth Row:
  1st, Brown glaze individual teapot (**T** on top of **M;** gold)   10.00- 12.50
  2nd, Brown glazed teapot w/floral design (embossed and
    yellow)   20.00- 22.50
  3rd, Individual brown glaze teapot (M in circle; white)
    with lid   6.00- 8.00

TEA or COFFEE POTS and SETS (Cont.)

Although the cup in the first row is similar to the rest of the pieces in that row, it is different and also marked differently. It was purchased with the set, but upon closer examination it is not the same. The coffee, creamer and sugar are marked in blue; "Sok China" with a basket in a wreath while the cup and saucer are in red MIOJ.

While the top rows on this page are fine porcelain, the pieces on the left and right in the bottom row are pottery.

The china demitasse cup and saucer in the bottom row is shown as a set on a wire rack in the First Series of my Occupied Japan book. For those of you who have been unable to find it, my publisher is going to reprint it. Check the last page of this book for price information.

You can expect to pay a premium (more than the sum of the pieces) if you find a complete set!

Top Row:
1st, Luster ware floral demitasse set (red)	$ 10.00- 12.50
2nd, Tea set consisting of six cup/saucers, creamer, sugar and teapot ("Sok China"; basket in wreath emblem; blue)	75.00-100.00
Creamer	8.00- 10.00
Sugar w/lid	10.00- 12.50
Teapot	25.00- 30.00
Cup and saucer (not pictured)	6.00- 7.00

Second Row:
Pink floral set on green background consisting of six each cup/saucers and 5½" plates, creamer, sugar and teapot (elephant head w/**A**)	175.00-225.00
Creamer	10.00- 12.50
Sugar w/lid	15.00- 17.50
Teapot	50.00- 60.00
Cup and saucer	10.00- 12.50
Plate	6.00- 8.00

Third Row:
Floral w/ivy set consisting of four cup/saucers creamer, sugar and teapot (**M S** on shield inside wreath, H.P.; red)	100.00-125.00
Creamer	8.00- 10.00
Sugar w/lid	12.50- 15.00
Teapot	35.00- 40.00
Cup and saucer	10.00- 12.00

Fourth Row:
1st, Demitasse set, floral pottery	8.00- 10.00
2nd, Sugar w/lid, floral pottery ("Morikin Ware"; blue)	10.00- 12.50
3rd, Red bird teapot (red)	25.00- 35.00
4th, Demitasse cup/saucer (**S.G.K.** in diamond; red)	8.00- 9.00
Set for six w/stand	50.00- 60.00
5th, Individual teapot (red)	12.50- 15.00

TOYS

The toys in the next three photographs are the largest selection I have been able to garner for pictures in any of my four books. Most toys are in the original box, but prices are listed for the toys without the box. **Add 10% to 20% for boxed toys depending upon the condition of the box.**

Most of the toys still are in working condition. Many of these are approaching, or have already passed, forty years of age. Not many cheaply made American toys work forty days later ... let alone forty years! Most of those shown here are wind-ups.

Some of the more interesting toys include: "Auto cycle" in the second row; "Sparking Loop Plane" and "Remote Control Car" in the third row and the "Circus Tricycle" in the fourth row. The "Auto Cycle" was, for me, a new name for a motorcycle. The "Sparking Loop Plane" does exactly that when wound up and let loose. The "Remote Control Car" has a steering wheel attached to a wire that you turn to control the car. I bet that was a very popular car with kids at the time. The "Circus Tricycle" does wheelies!

A special thanks to Fred Finkel, a dealer in toys, who helped with toy prices.

Top Row:
    1st, "Hopping Dog" (impressed in metal base; MIOJ on box) $15.00- 17.50
    2nd, "Cowboy w/Two Guns" (embossed on back; box marked
        M on top of **T** { Modern Toy} Pat #1157)   40.00- 45.00
    3rd, Celluloid "Toddling Babe" (embossed on back; box
        marked w/**TOY** written in large **N**, Mechanco Toy)   50.00- 60.00

Second Row:
    1st, "Playing Dog" (impressed mark on shoe; MIOJ on box)   45.00- 55.00
    2nd, "Monkey Sweet Melodian" (embossed on back **M** on top
        of **T**; box MIOJ #5308)   60.00- 75.00
    3rd, Celluloid swan on box but looks like chick (embossed on
        tail; propeller symbol)   20.00- 22.50
    4th, "Auto cycle" ("Showa" in emblem on base; **T.N.** in
        diamond on toy)   300.00-350.00

Third Row:
    1st, "Sparking Loop Plane" (**M** on top of **T** on box; same
        mark under wing of plane)   125.00-150.00
    2nd, "Penguin" (impressed on wing; box MIOJ "Alps" with
        mountains)   30.00- 40.00
    3rd, "Remote Control Car" (impressed on base; box **T.N.** in
        diamond, Itako Trade Mark, MIOJ)   75.00-100.00

Fourth Row:
    1st, "Camel" (paper label; box MIOJ)   65.00- 80.00
    2nd, Small car   20.00- 25.00
    3rd, Celluloid "Cheery Cook" (embossed w/**TOY** written in
        large **N**, Mechanco Toy on back)   50.00- 60.00
    4th, Celluloid boy "Circus Tricycle" (embossed on back;
        box #385 MIOJ)   55.00- 65.00

Fifth Row:
    1st, Inflatable football (stamped "Cherry" MIOJ)   20.00- 22.50
    2nd and 3rd, Inflatable rabbits (stamped on foot)   15.00- 17.50 ea.

TOYS – WIND-UPS

The names of these wind-ups can not be ascertained since I do not have the boxes for them. I'm sure that some of them are named. The giraffe in the fourth row was packed two to a box, but the boxes are plain.

Add 10% to 20% for boxed toys depending upon the condition of the box.

Top Row:

1st, Monkey on tricycle (impressed in metal on side of cycle)	$ 75.00-100.00
2nd, Monkey tips hat and wiggles tail (embossed on back)	40.00- 50.00
3rd, Celluloid baseball catcher rolls looking for pop-up (impressed on green between legs)	65.00- 75.00
4th, Metal dog munching hat w/circling tail (stamped on bottom)	40.00- 50.00
5th, Celluloid clown monkey flips over on hands (embossed on foot)	55.00- 65.00
6th, Celluloid xylophone player (impressed on base)	90.00-110.00

Second Row:

1st, Celluloid rabbit pulling metal wagon w/celluloid egg and ducks (impressed in metal)	75.00-100.00
2nd, Walking camel (paper label on fur coat)	45.00- 55.00
3rd, Walking metal duck (impressed on foot)	20.00- 25.00
4th, Flipping celluloid clown (embossed on back)	50.00- 60.00

Third Row:

1st, Metal tricycle missing rider (impressed on side)	15.00- 17.50
2nd, Celluloid boy w/metal case hops up and down ("Paris" on metal case and embossed on boy)	50.00- 60.00
3rd, Wind-up car 5" (impressed mark on base)	50.00- 60.00
4th, Celluloid flipping monkey (embossed on back)	40.00- 50.00
5th, Wind-up car 3" (impressed mark on base)	25.00- 30.00

Fourth Row:

1st, Hopping "Rudolph" reindeer (stamped on metal)	50.00- 60.00
2nd, Celluloid walking Santa (embossed on back)	400.00-450.00
3rd, Roller skating bear (impressed on skate)	175.00-200.00
4th, Walking, hopping giraffe (impressed in metal)	40.00- 50.00
5th, Celluloid acrobatic gymnast (embossed on back and foot)	100.00-125.00

Fifth Row:

1st, Walking lion (paper label)	35.00- 45.00
2nd, Hopping dog w/bone (paper label)	35.00- 45.00
3rd, Walking elephant (paper label)	35.00- 45.00
4th, Walking dog (impressed in metal)	30.00- 35.00

TOYS – WIND-UPS (Cont.)

Add 10% to 20% for boxed toys depending upon the condition of the box.

Top Row:
    "Angora Rabbit" hops; three colors all found in same box
        (impressed on metal; box marked Japan) $ 15.00- 17.50 ea.

Second Row:
    1st, Hopping squirrel (paper label)   90.00-110.00
    2nd, "Finest Pearl Fur Toys Jumping Rabbit" (impressed
        mark on metal base of rabbit; box MIOJ, **M** on top **T**)   15.00- 17.50

Third Row:
    1st and 2nd, "Studebaker" (impressed on car; box MIOJ,
        Sinsei Toys Industrial Co., Ltd; **SKK** in diamond)   60.00- 75.00 ea.
    3rd, "Baby Pontiac" (impressed on car; box **M** on top **T**)   40.00- 45.00
    4th, "Chevrolet with Back Motion" (impressed on car; box
        MIOJ; **SKK** in diamond)   50.00- 60.00

Fourth Row:
    1st, "Sarcus" celluloid elephant spinning barrel on metal
        ball (embossed on back; box MIOJ, Suzuki Trade Mark)   300.00-350.00
    2nd, "Circus Elephant" balances on front feet (embossed
        Japan on ball; box Japan **KSK** in diamond)   275.00-325.00
    3rd, "Sarcus" celluloid monkey spinning die on barrel on
        metal ball (embossed on back; box MIOJ, Suzuki Trade
        Mark)   300.00-350.00

Fifth Row:
    1st, Celluloid "Cowboy" spins rope (embossed on back
        under gun belt)   65.00- 75.00
    2nd, "Trick Seal" w/celluloid ball (impressed in metal base;
        box Pat #15204 Trade Mark Alps {mountain symbols}
        MIOJ)   50.00- 65.00
    3rd, Celluloid pink seal w/celluloid ball (embossed on side
        by flipper)   50.00- 65.00

VASES

As you can see from more than eighty vases shown in the next two pages, the multitude of Occupied Japan vases vary not only in size, but also in quality. Many of the designs are intricate and colorful, while others were void of color and imagination.

In the top row are two "Ucagco China" vases with open lattice work and floral decorations. These vases would add to anyone's decor today, and you could purchase them for about the same as you could a new one. At least the Occupied Japan would have a collectible value behind it. The new one would be discarded in a few years at a garage or estate sale or even the local flea market for ten or fifteen per cent of the price paid for it, but the Occupied Japan would probably bring as much or more than was paid for it.

Quality made Occupied Japan items make great gifts; but make sure the recipient understands that it is a collectible and not a piece of "junque!"

Top Row:

1st, Vase w/floral decoration, 8" ("Ucagco China" w/emblem; gold)	$35.00-40.00
2nd, Same as 1st, except 6"	25.00-30.00
3rd, Cornucopia (brown)	12.50-15.00
4th, Pottery vase w/blue windmills (blue)	17.50-20.00
5th, Raised rose bud vase (red)	8.00-10.00
6th, Cylinder vase with island scene, 8"	25.00-35.00

Second Row:

1st, Floral two-handled, 4⅞"	6.00- 8.00
2nd, Rust floral "Niagara Cave, Harmony Minn." (red)	8.00-10.00
3rd and 4th, Cornucopias w/floral design	6.00- 8.00 ea.
5th, Two-handled floral (red)	5.00- 6.00
6th, Pottery decorated (embossed)	15.00-17.50
7th, Orange floral (red)	6.00- 7.50
8th, Blue floral (red)	8.00-10.00

Third Row:

1st, Floral, 2⅝"	2.00- 3.00
2nd, Tulip (red)	2.00- 3.00
3rd, Blue open handled	2.50- 4.00
4th-8th, Mini vases (red)	2.00- 3.00 ea.
9th, Windmill design	4.00- 5.00
10th, Floral (red)	2.00- 3.00
11th, Spatter ware (brown)	6.00- 8.00
12th, Embossed children, 3"	8.00-10.00

Fourth Row:

1st, Green floral, 3⅞" (red)	7.50-10.00
2nd, Blue w/pink flower	6.00- 8.00
3rd, Orange flower (red)	7.50-10.00
4th, Footed vase (red)	5.00- 6.00
5th, Mexican siesta (red)	10.00-12.50
6th-9th, Brown vases	4.00- 5.00 ea.

Fifth Row:

1st-7th, Brown vases, 3¾" to 4"	6.00- 8.00 ea.
8th and 9th, Brown vases	4.00- 5.00 ea.

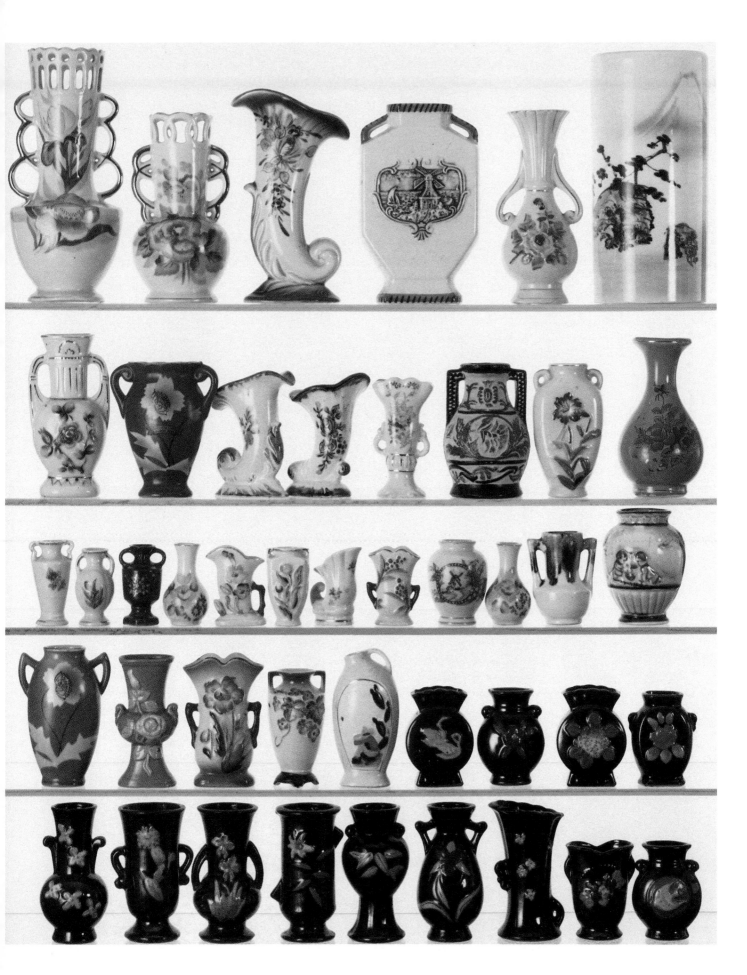

VASES (Cont.)

Many of the figurine vases shown here were used in other capacities. One of the favorite ways these were used wa to add material to the opening and make a pin cushion out of it. There is more collector interest in the figurine vas styles than there are the other types shown on the previous page.

Top Row:

1st, Girl w/apron opening, 4⅞" (red)	$10.00-12.50
2nd, Same, only 3⅞"	8.00-10.00
3rd, Chinese boy in vase, 6⅛" (red)	25.00-30.00
4th, Colonial lady in vase (red)	25.00-30.00
5th, Two-handled child (red)	15.00-17.50
6th, Colonial man, 3¼" (red)	5.00- 6.00
7th, Child w/basket	7.50-10.00

Second Row:

1st, Oriental lad, 4½" (red)	12.50-15.00
2nd, Oriental lady (red)	15.00-17.50
3rd, Cowboy w/cactus (red)	12.50-15.00
4th, Boy w/accordion	5.00- 6.00
5th, "Hummel" type boy w/violin	15.00-17.50
6th, Girl	8.00-10.00

Third Row:

1st, Colonial girl, 2½"	2.50- 4.00
2nd, Clown w/egg	12.50-15.00
3rd, Brown vase	4.00- 5.00
4th, Boy w/cart	5.00- 6.00
5th, Colonial by flower (red)	5.00- 6.00
6th, Mexican by cactus (blue)	5.00- 6.00
7th and 8th, Colonials	4.00- 5.00 ea.

Fourth Row:

1st and 2nd, Colonial lady or man, 3½" (red)	6.00- 8.00 ea.
3rd, Vase w/dancer (red)	8.00-10.00
4th, Child (red)	4.00- 5.00
5th, Lady w/blue basket (red)	4.00- 5.00
6th, Pottery-like vase (embossed)	5.00- 6.00
7th-9th, Lady or man, 2" (red)	2.50- 4.00 ea.

Fifth Row:

1st and 2nd, Brown or orange vase, 2½" (crown emblem; red)	5.00- 6.00 ea.
3rd-6th, Oriental vases, 2½" (red)	5.00- 6.00 ea.
7th, Oriental (red H.P.)	7.50-10.00
8th and 9th, Oriental w/green or yellow rim, 2½"	5.00- 6.00 ea.

UNUSUAL, LARGE and COVER DESCRIPTION

Here are some of the largest and best of the items found for this book. The listing for the pieces on the cover is als
shown here since several of these pieces were not shown previously in this book. The cover pictures for **two** book
were photographed at the same time and some of the pieces on the cover will be shown later in my fifth book.

Page 125

Top Row:

1st and 2nd, Oriental couple, 10½"	$100.00-125.00 pr.
3rd, Bamboo mat (stamped in middle of wood)	20.00- 25.00

Bottom Row:

1st, Needle point "1946 Occupied Commemoration in Japan - In Tokyo"	200.00-250.00
2nd, Musketeer, 17¼" (**S.G.K.** basket in wreath MIOJ)	200.00-300.00

Page 126

Clock (Trade mark Occupied Japan w/horse jumping over world; MIOJ at bottom face of clock also)	300.00-350.00

Page 127

Cover description:

Left foreground; bird cage clock (impressed)	150.00-200.00
Left background; musician couple, 10⅛"	125.00-150.00 pr.
Center foreground; china inkwell ("Andrea, H.P.")	60.00- 75.00
Center; tea set ("Ucagco China" w/emblem; gold)	75.00-100.00
Teapot	40.00- 50.00
Creamer	15.00- 17.50
Sugar w/lid	20.00- 25.00
Center background; musketeer, 17¼" (**S.G.K.** basket in wreath MIOJ)	200.00-300.00
Right foreground; souvenir china casserole ("Meito Norleans China Centennial"; gold); lid marked inside top -"Commemorating 100 Years of Service, United China & Glass Co., New Orleans U.S.A. 1850-1950"	50.00- 65.00
Right background; Cinderella and Prince Charming, 8¼" ("Maruyama"; red)	75.00-100.00

Schroeder's Antiques Price Guide

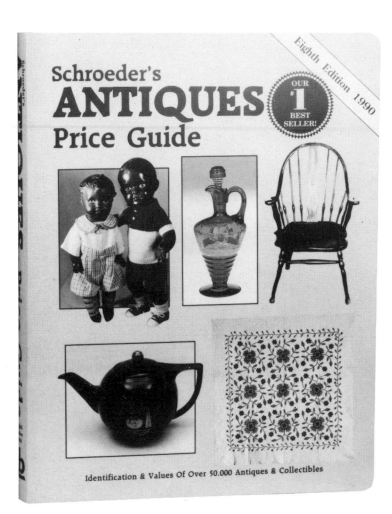

Schroeder's Antiques Price Guide has climbed its way to the top in a field already supplied with several well-established publications! The word is out, *Schroeder's Price Guide* is the best buy at any price. Over 500 categories are covered, with more than 50,000 listings. But it's not volume alone that makes Schroeder's the unique guide it is recognized to be. From ABC Plates to Zsolnay, if it merits the interest of today's collector, you'll find it in Schroeder's. Each subject is represented with histories and background information. In addition, hundreds of sharp original photos are used each year to illustrate not only the rare and the unusual, but the everyday "fun-type" collectibles as well -- not postage stamp pictures, but large close-up shots that show important details clearly.

Each edition is completely re-typeset from all new sources. We have not and will not simply change prices in each new edition. All new copy and all new illustrations make Schroeder's THE price guide on antiques and collectibles.

The writing and researching team behind this giant is proportionately large. It is backed by a staff of more than seventy of Collector Books' finest authors, as well as a board of advisors made up of well-known antique authorities and the country's top dealers, all specialists in their fields. Accuracy is their primary aim. Prices are gathered over the entire year previous to publication, from ads and personal contacts. Then each category is thoroughly checked to spot inconsistencies, listings that may not be entirely reflective of actual market dealings, and lines too vague to be of merit.

Only the best of the lot remains for publication. You'll find *Schroeder's Antiques Price Guide* the one to buy for factual information and quality.

No dealer, collector or investor can afford not to own this book. It is available from your favorite bookseller or antiques dealer at the low price of $12.95. If you are unable to find this price guide in your area, it's available from Collector Books, P. O. Box 3009, Paducah, KY 42001 at $12.95 plus $2.00 for postage and handling.

8½ x 11, 608 Pages $12.95

COLLECTOR BOOKS
A Division of Schroeder Publishing Co., Inc.